Praise for *Coffee with Jesus*

"The cheeky, online comic strip that has gained a cult audience of 40,000-plus followers in less than three years is now ready to burst upon the world as a giftable, brightly hued coffee-table book. . . . The wit is barbed, theology surprisingly relevant, and the overall effect highly addictive."

JOHN MURASKI, Religion News Service

> Why are people always surprised that I'm relevant?

"David Wilkie accomplishes in a four-panel comic strip what preachers try to achieve in a 45-minute sermon—making one solid point that delivers a spiritual truth."

JEFF FRIEND, *Worship Leader* magazine

> If it takes you 45 minutes, you might be doing it wrong.

"The heart is the comic collection and its humor, at once gentle and barbed and more thought-provoking than many a sermon. Buy this for a Christmas gift, to be read over a cup of strong joe."

Publishers Weekly

"Irreverent yet insightful."

HEIDI SCHLUMPF, *National Catholic Reporter*

Brought to you by Radio Free Babylon and InterVarsity Press

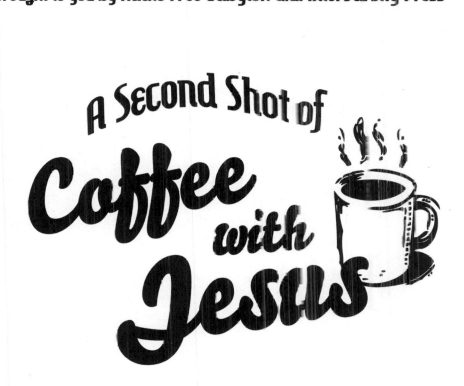

A Second Shot of Coffee with Jesus

David Wilkie

IVP Books

An imprint of InterVarsity Press
Downers Grove, Illinois

InterVarsity Press
P.O. Box 1400, Downers Grove, IL 60515-1426
ivpress.com
email@ivpress.com

InterVarsity Press® is the book-publishing division of InterVarsity Christian Fellowship/USA®, a movement of students and faculty active on campus at hundreds of universities, colleges and schools of nursing in the United States of America, and a member movement of the International Fellowship of Evangelical Students. For information about local and regional activities, visit intervarsity.org.

Cover design: Cindy Kiple
Images: Woodgrain background: ©DonVanover/iStockphoto
     Cover Illustrations: ©Dave Wilke

ISBN 978-0-8308-3693-2 (print)
ISBN 978-0-8308-9760-5 (digital)

Printed in the United States of America ♾

g green press As a member of the Green Press Initiative, InterVarsity Press is committed to protecting the environment and to the responsible use **INITIATIVE** of natural resources. To learn more, visit greenpressinitiative.org.

Library of Congress Cataloging-in-Publication Data

A catalog record for this book is available from the Library of Congress.

P	25	24	23	22	21	20	19	18	17	16	15	14	13	12	11	10	9	8	7	6	5	4	3	2	1
Y	37	36	35	34	33	32	31	30	29	28	27	26	25	24	23	22	21	20	19	18	17	16	15		

For Joe.

I saw you *talking to God*.

I wanted that.

Contents

Acknowledgments / 9

Introduction / 11

A Second Shot of Coffee with Jesus / 13

About Radio Free Babylon / 127

Acknowledgments

Were you on that list of acknowledgments in the first *Coffee with Jesus* book? Then consider yourself thanked again. But special shout-outs to the following:

Joy, for her late-night slogging and help in laying out many of these strips; Al at IVP, for taking over where Dave ("Clark Kent") Zimmerman left off; Laura at IVP, for helping to smooth the process with her super-organized, super-sized, much-improved-on-the-original templates; Katie, for not settling when the comics didn't make her laugh or think, sending me back to the drawing board.

And I suppose I owe not a small bit of thanks to the intrusive, time-wasting, worldwide distraction that is Facebook. Most of you holding this book would not be doing so were it not for the help of Mark Zuckerberg and his army of evil geniuses bent on world domination.

Introduction

If there's one thing I've learned from reading the online comments on *Coffee with Jesus* comic strips (other than it's not a good idea to read online comments), it's that there are a lot of interpretations of who Jesus is. We tend to create him in our own image. To some, he's just sunshine and peace and rainbows and puppies, and he would never say the things he says in these strips. To some, he's a great philosopher who deserves respect. To others, he's an insecure and angry deity who will surely make me pay in some horrible manner for the way in which I've depicted him here.

To many, he's just a made-up story created by power-mad people to keep you in line. I hope it's clear in these comics who he is to me. Imitators have spawned online, creating what I consider rude and inaccurate portrayals of Jesus. If you've come across any of those, I hope it was easy to discern that they did not come from me.

The theology in these strips is fairly orthodox, though I might put a twist on what many consider orthodoxy. Jesus is practical, down-to-earth and real, but he's also the miracle-working Son of God. He's a whisper away, but he doesn't always whisper. He's got an opinion and he's not afraid to share it with the characters he encounters.

I did a few interviews after the first book was published. One interviewer, who I think was of the Sunshine Puppy School, stated, "Some of these are a little preachy." Well . . . *yeah!* Kinda comes with the territory. Jesus was a preacher. He stepped on toes. He skewered sacred cows. He pulled no punches. That's part of his love for us.

This collection of the comics will be treated a little differently than the first. You won't be subjected to any of my lyrics, nor will you have to suffer through any of my preachy essays. (Stop cheering already.) Instead, just enjoy the comics. Each one hopefully delivers a lesson, or maybe a laugh—in the best cases, both. This book is the kind you can pick up, flip to any page, read a couple of strips and then throw back on the nightstand. Or the coffee table. Or the toilet tank. Or, you can read them all in one sitting. And then hopefully read them again. They're created to encourage you, to challenge you, to amuse you and sometimes to make you stop and go, "Huh?"—which will hopefully then lead you to your own investigation.

Caution: Contents are hot. Best savored slowly.

Enjoy.

Peace,
Dave Wilkie
Wekiva Springs, Florida

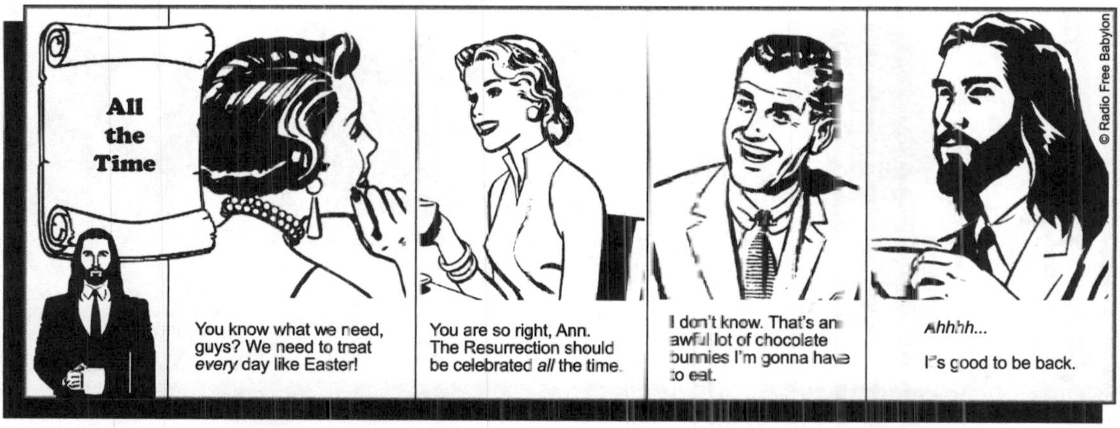
All the Time
© Radio Free Babylon
You know what we need, guys? We need to treat *every* day like Easter!
You are so right, Ann. The Resurrection should be celebrated *all* the time.
I don't know. That's an awful lot of chocolate bunnies I'm gonna have to eat.
Ahhhh...
It's good to be back.

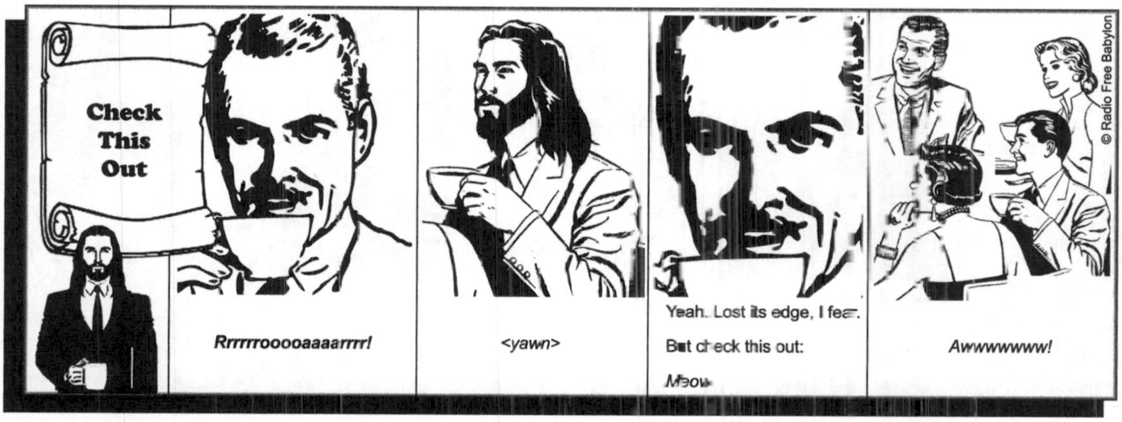
Check This Out
© Radio Free Babylon
Rrrrrroooaaaarrrr!
<yawn>
Yeah. Lost its edge, I fear.
But check this out:
Meow.
Awwwwwww!

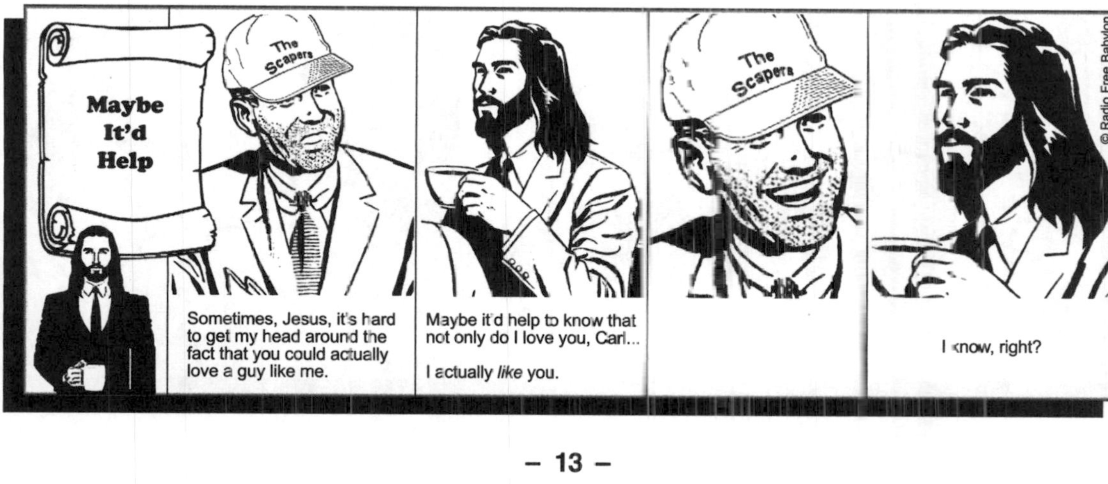
Maybe It'd Help
© Radio Free Babylon
The Scapera
Sometimes, Jesus, it's hard to get my head around the fact that you could actually love a guy like me.
Maybe it'd help to know that not only do I love you, Carl...
I actually *like* you.
The Scapera
I know, right?

Gorging on Candy

You know how in the cartoons there's a little angel on one shoulder and a little devil on the other, Jesus?

Sure, Ann. Representing your capacity to choose to do right or wrong.

Well, I don't hear much from the little angel these days, while the little devil seems to be shouting.

One is fatigued from lack of food while the other is like a toddler gorging on candy.

Try switching their diets.

© Radio Free Babylon

Feel-Good Fest

I think everyone really liked yesterday's sermon. I had quite a few come up to me after the service to say so.

People love to hear what they want to hear, Joe. It was a real feel-good fest.

Uhhh...you sound like you didn't care for it.

OK, give it to me straight.

If Oprah and Osteen had a child together and named it Tony Robbins, that was your sermon yesterday.

© Radio Free Babylon

Too Familiar

You think this culture is getting too familiar with you, J-Man? Making you more "friend" than Lord?

Some humanize me to the point that they forget I'm God, sure; but just as easily others forget that I'm equally human, Carl.

Do I have balance, J-Man?

Lord...

Lord J-Man?

You sometimes confuse "friend" with "buddy," Carl.

So, no, I'm not meeting you at Hooters for lunch.

© Radio Free Babylon

Roller Coaster

My life feels like a roller coaster, Jesus. It's up and down, wild turns, climbing slowly or plummeting rapidly. It's frightening!

You know how they lower that steel bar when you get into the roller coaster, Lisa? That thing you grip, that keeps you secure?

Yeah, sure.

I'm the steel bar.

What We Believe

When a church changes its name from, say, "St. Mark's First Congregational Baptist Assembly" to the more inviting "Pine Valley Church"...

I get it, Kevin. Your skills in marketing are legendary. If you hide the denominational affiliation, you can get past some built-in prejudices.

Exactly. And we discovered that only fourteen percent of newcomers will bother to investigate the "What We Believe" part of the website.

Sort of like the nutrition label on a bag of Doritos.

Fish Magnet

My pastor says we should share our faith, Jesus, but people don't really want to hear me talk about it.

Well, your little fish magnet on the back of your truck has won a total of...let me count...zero souls, Carl.

So, now you're against fish magnets, Jesus?

Man, you can be harsh.

Fish, Carl.

And be a magnet.

War Being Waged

I get so angry, Jesus, when I hear these smart-mouthed comedians mocking people of faith. There's a war being waged against Christians!

Did you know, Ann, that tens of thousands of people are killed each year simply because they believe in me?

Oh, my.

So, like...*real* war.

Yeah. So if the cost of your discipleship means Bill Maher makes fun of you, Ann?

Wow.

Making a Dent

If I spoke with a Scottish accent, I bet I'd get more people in this church, Jesus.

It's true that people are suckers for a rich brogue, Joe. But how about you just be Joe?

Just plain old Joe, toiling in obscurity, making a tiny dent for the kingdom.

You're fixing dents and straightening frames. It's like...

Joe's Body Shop!

More Spiritual

I want to combine my faith in you with a sort of Kabbalah-Buddhist-Yoga-Zen thing, Jesus...if that's OK.

What's lacking in your current faith that makes you want to seek these paths, Lisa?

I don't know. Those other paths just seem more...more *spiritual*, ya know?

Said the woman within whom dwells the Spirit of the Creator of all that is, seen and unseen.

Try Loving Them

I think Christianity is in retreat mode, Jesus. We've surrendered the high ground. We're letting them win when we should be attacking!

As long as you're imagining enemies around every corner, Kevin, maybe you can try loving them.

I wish it were that easy Jesus! Even *identifying* as a Christian is now viewed *negatively* in this society! When did *that* happen?

Like around 33 AD, Kevin.

Awww, Mom!

When your mom told you they'd run out of wine, why did you say, *"Woman, what have I to do with you?"* That seems a little rude, Jesus.

You have to imagine the tone, Carl. It was more like *"Awww, Mom!"* There was no disrespect in it at all.

I can totally see it. The reluctant son is gently urged into his life's work by his faithful mother.

For a few weeks after that, I disappointed quite a few business consultants wanting me to start Wedding Catering by Jesus.

Angels

It's weird to think that all around us, all the time, is another dimension, Jesus; of angels and helpers, and even fallen angels!

There's a lot going on that most people never give a thought to, Ann.

My mother used to tell me that I had my own personal guardian angel.

Your mom was being sweet. There've been times, Ann, when you've required an entire battalion.

Jesus Did it All

The preachers say, "You can't do anything! Jesus did it all!" *Then* they say, "You *have* to do A, B and C." Or, "You *can't* do X, Y or Z."

If you died tomorrow, Carl, where do you suppose you'd stand with me?

You'd let me into paradise.

I'm saved by grace through faith in you, aren't I?

Correct, Carl!

Now live like it.

© Radio Free Babylon

Big Jackpot

I'll bet you're fielding a lot of requests from people praying they win the big jackpot tomorrow, Jesus.

Oh, bunches; from people I haven't heard from in years, from people I don't even know, all promising to do great works with the cash.

Well, you *know* I'd give ten percent...at least! I mean, if I should be so lucky. Um, I mean blessed. That is, if it's your will, Jesus.

Yeah, Lisa. It's not.

© Radio Free Babylon

Humility

I've been trying to work on my humility, Jesus.

I'm getting a lot better!

<In three...two...one>

Crap!

I'm actually *proud* of that!

Humbling, isn't it?

© Radio Free Babylon

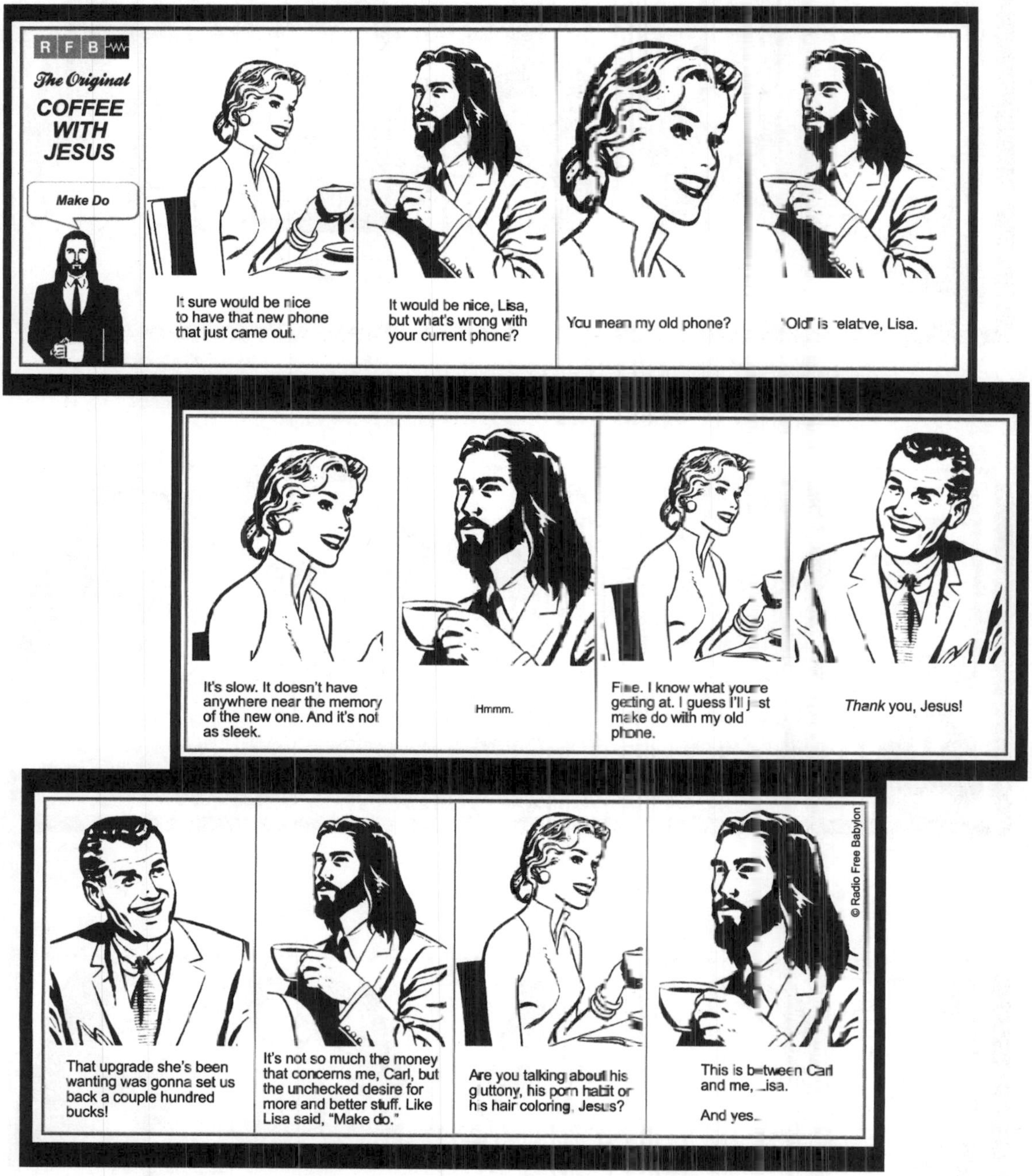
RFB
The Original
COFFEE WITH JESUS
Make Do
It sure would be nice to have that new phone that just came out.
It would be nice, Lisa, but what's wrong with your current phone?
You mean my old phone?
"Old" is relative, Lisa.
It's slow. It doesn't have anywhere near the memory of the new one. And it's not as sleek.
Hmmm.
Fine. I know what you're getting at. I guess I'll just make do with my old phone.
Thank you, Jesus!
That upgrade she's been wanting was gonna set us back a couple hundred bucks!
It's not so much the money that concerns me, Carl, but the unchecked desire for more and better stuff. Like Lisa said, "Make do."
Are you talking about his gluttony, his porn habit or his hair coloring, Jesus?
This is between Carl and me, Lisa.
And yes.
© Radio Free Babylon

Amen

Is it pronounced *ay*-men, Jesus, or *ah*-men?

Is my name Jesus, Joe? Or is it Jésus, Isa, Ιησούς, Gesù, Ježíš, Иисус, Jesús, Jézus, Jezi or Yeshua?

I don't think it matters, Jesus. Whatever we call you, you're the same.

Amen.

Those Who Weep

What are you doing with all those "thoughts and prayers" and "hearts going out" to the tornado victims, Son of Man?

I hear them, Satan.

I grieve with them.

I comfort them.

Well, I for one am having a *spectacular* week! So many people questioning why you let this happen!

And while you debate the laws of nature, my people and I will be weeping with those who weep.

Lover of Self

I was reading an article in *Self* magazine, Jesus, about how I could get my perfect beach body in just six days.

Please, Lisa, don't be a lover of *Self*.

I know, I know.

But I don't think it's wrong to simply want to look your best.

Well, surely they can't mean a *literal* six days.

Cut-Throat

I'll be taking you into some pretty ugly situations and uncomfortable meetings today at work, Jesus.

Awesome, Ann!

I hate it when you leave me in the parking lot.

Things are cut-throat in there, Jesus. People get stabbed in the back, cut off at the knees.

So I'll get to say, "Ann, put away your sword!" quite a few times today.

© Radio Free Babylon

Hidden Prophecies

It's so cool, Jesus, how you included all these hidden prophecies within the Bible that are found through secret codes.

That everyone seems to uncover *after* the fact, Kevin.

Not so! Well before the last election we saw clues in Deuteronomy 28:13-14 clearly showing Romney would become president.

Oh, well then, there you go.

© Radio Free Babylon

Atrocities

Why do atheists hate you so much, Jesus?

You can't hate what you don't believe in, Carl. They hate the atrocities done in my name.

Crusades? Inquisition? That sort of stuff?

That stuff, sure. But also *Holy Land Experience* in Orlando, the *Left Behind* series, the Christian music industry. Want me to go on?

© Radio Free Babylon

Money, Fame, Power, Sex

I see these stars on the red carpet and in the magazines, Jesus, and I can't help it, but I get envious! I want what they have!

All that money, fame, power, sex; the good tables at the best restaurants; none of that will ever take the place of the peace of God, Lisa.

You're not saying that famous, glamorous people can't have what they have AND be considered among your followers, are you?

No, but it is easier for a camel to pass through security at LAX than it is for a celebrity to get his driver to find my place. Yeah...something like that.

A Little Addendum

Do you mind if I tack on a little addendum to the *"give us this day our daily bread"* line?

Carl, I know where you're going with this, and by *"daily bread,"* I didn't mean *"the winning lottery ticket."*

C'mon, J-Man! You know I'll spend it right! Think of all the good things I can do for you with all that money!

It's you pulling up to one of your orphanages or homeless shelters in one of your rare Lamborghinis where the picture starts to get weird.

Power of Pride

The more your people secretly delight in their superiority, the stronger my hold on them, Son of Man. It's ridiculously simple!

It's a wicked game you play, Satan, and you're quite good at it. And many of them don't even bother to conceal their delight anymore.

The Power of Pride!

Yeah, but look where it got you: a temp job in a sweatshop with no chance of advancement.

Gloss and Dross

You can gauge my progress with this culture simply by looking at the magazines in the check-out lines at the supermarkets, Son of Man.

Lurid celebrity gossip, an obsession with style and image, and a fascination with Nostradamus and the end times

Yes! Yes! All this superficial gloss and dross, and yet a fear of the end! *But the best part?* All the fear with none of the repentance!

A Great Awakening sometimes follows a disturbing nightmare, Satan. Go ahead and delight in the cause, but the effect is going to drive you mad.

Stagnant Swamp

I've been looking back on my youth, Jesus. If I only knew then what I know now...

Look forward, Ann. Regret is a stagnant swamp full of weeds, insects, and large biting reptiles. Quit wallowing in the stench and scum.

Gross. You make me feel like I need a bath.

I know of a clear, cool river that will do a better job.

We Rebuke You

I just love it when your people interrupt their prayers to you to address me boldly, Son of Man, announcing, *"And Satan! We rebuke you!"*

Dangerously bold, I'm afraid.

It's like they've never heard the verse, *"Resist the devil and he will flee from you."* Their attention is just so *delicious! I crave it!*

You're like the Hollywood star relishing momentary fame from a sex tape, Satan. Enjoy the attention while it lasts.

Day of Judgment

So, Jesus, in the day of judgment, *everything we ever did* is going to be revealed?

Everything, Carl.

And yes, even your browsing history.

Yeah, it's not gonna be pretty.

Waste This Day

Jesus, please don't let me waste this day.

Don't waste this day, Lisa.

Wait, you can't do that.

Now the pressure's on me!

Just taking off the training wheels, Lisa.

I'll jog alongside in case you lose your balance.

Great Moral Teacher

You were a great moral teacher, Son of Man.

Let's just leave it at that.

Nice try, Satan, but you have to take into account all of my words, not just what you consider the "great moral teachings."

What?

That you are the *Christ?*

The Son of the Living God?

Word.

Painful Charade

Some people put on their best faces when I'm around, Jesus. It's like they're acting.

You're a reminder to those people, Joe, that the life they say they live isn't the one they really do.

It's like this painful charade. It's *so* fake.

Welcome to my world, Joe.

Real Riffraff

Ugh. Some renters moved in a couple houses down, Jesus. Not to judge, but they look to be real riffraff. This is gonna hurt property values.

Riffraff, you say?

They sound like my kind of people, Carl.

<sigh>

So, what...cookies? Maybe brownies?

That's what I'm talkin' about, son!

Cast Them Out

You know those movies, Jesus, where the family is trying to fight off demons, ghosts or aliens or whatever has invaded their house?

Sure, Ann.

How come the family never thinks to just trust in you, or call on you to cast them out?

Be a pretty short movie.

Properly Grieve

I haven't been this down since my divorce, Jesus. I can barely function. I walk through the day glassy-eyed, numb, just listless.

Snap out of it, Kevin.

Wish I could. Maybe I just need to take a few days off to properly grieve.

Bereavement leave is for members of your immediate family, Kevin, not characters on *Game of Thrones*.

A Hundred Times

I was telling a friend about you, Jesus, and she just shut me down, saying, *"I don't need a savior, Lisa!"*

She's heard the message a hundred times, Lisa.

She runs from it now.

Wow. So there's no hope.

On the contrary, Lisa.

When you're as dogged as I am, people eventually turn around to confront you.

Live in Fear

I know you see it, Son of Man. The rudeness, the anger, the anxiety, the depression! Isn't it just *divine?*

You see what you want to see, Satan.

And no, it's not divine.

Oh, come now, Boy King. I hear your people praying.

Even *they* live in fear!

Sometimes, but the world's a scary place, life is hard and they're human.

What's your excuse?

So Long Ago

Your very last words in the Bible were, *"Yes, I am coming quickly,"* Jesus, but that was *soooo* long ago!

Long ago by your thinking, Kevin.

My promise is still good.

This is that *"a day is like a thousand years, and a thousand years are like a day"* excuse, isn't it?

And had I returned on your timetable, Kevin, you wouldn't even be here.

Sow a Seed

And he said if I "sowed a seed of faith," you'd bless that gift and increase it ten, a hundred, a thousand fold!

So you called the toll-free number, pledged some money, and now you're expecting me to give you a return on your investment.

Well those rates are a whole lot better than I can get at any bank, Jesus.

Did you happen to notice, Carl, that the man pitching this scheme was seated on a gold throne and wearing a three-thousand dollar suit?

What I Was Thinking

I had my car washed at the youth group fundraiser over at Worship World, Jesus.

I saw that, Joe. And you said hi to Pastor Steve and were very gracious.

I'm sure you also saw what I was thinking and how hard I was trying *not* to think it.

Well, Joe, it *is* a campus and he *is* a big man.

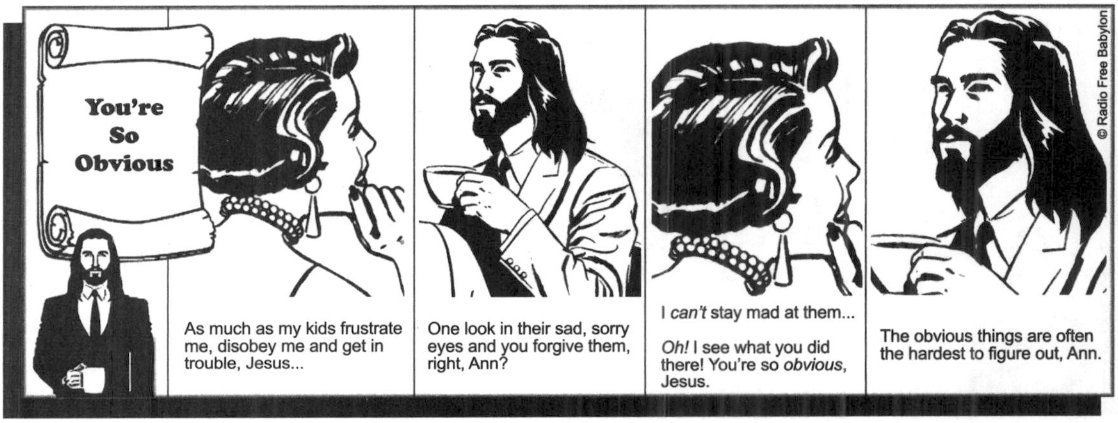
You're So Obvious
© Radio Free Babylon
As much as my kids frustrate me, disobey me and get in trouble, Jesus...
One look in their sad, sorry eyes and you forgive them, right, Ann?
I *can't* stay mad at them...
Oh! I see what you did there! You're so *obvious*, Jesus.
The obvious things are often the hardest to figure out, Ann.

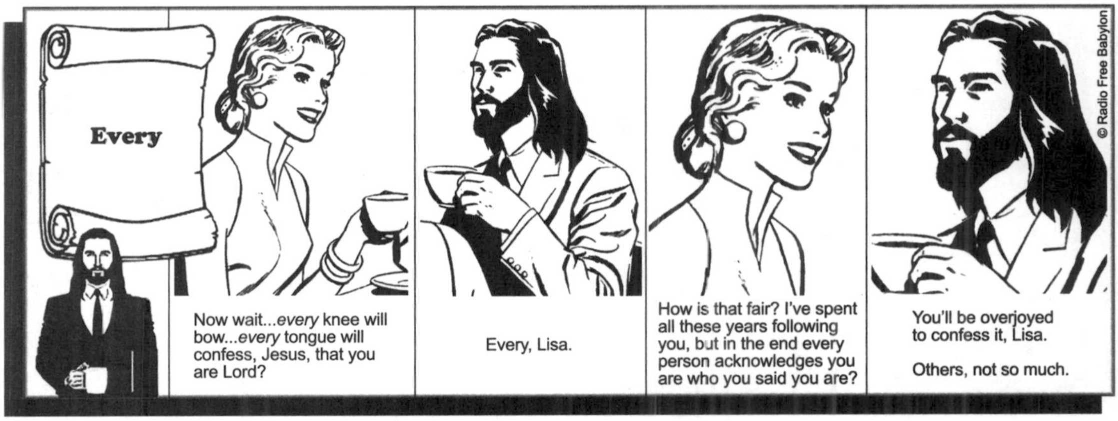
Every
© Radio Free Babylon
Now wait...*every* knee will bow...*every* tongue will confess, Jesus, that you are Lord?
Every, Lisa.
How is that fair? I've spent all these years following you, but in the end every person acknowledges you are who you said you are?
You'll be overjoyed to confess it, Lisa.
Others, not so much.

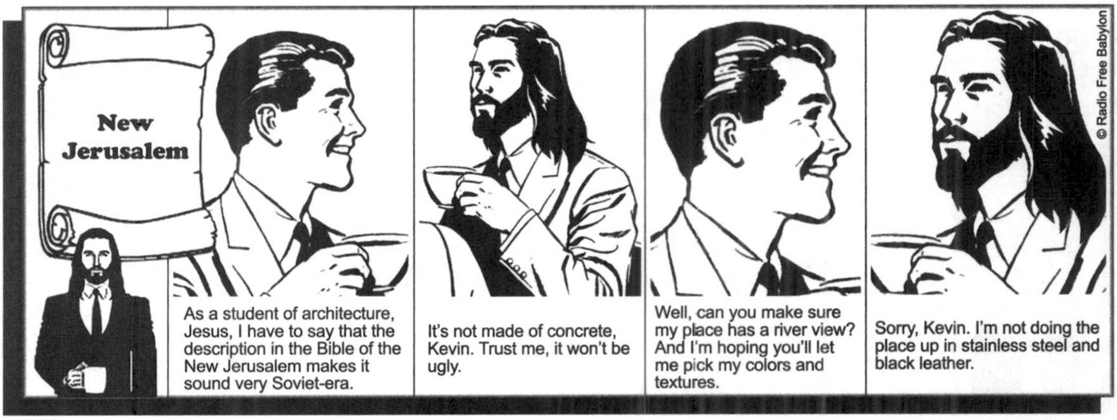
New Jerusalem
© Radio Free Babylon
As a student of architecture, Jesus, I have to say that the description in the Bible of the New Jerusalem makes it sound very Soviet-era.
It's not made of concrete, Kevin. Trust me, it won't be ugly.
Well, can you make sure my place has a river view? And I'm hoping you'll let me pick my colors and textures.
Sorry, Kevin. I'm not doing the place up in stainless steel and black leather.

That One Faction

That one faction of your followers, Jesus? They really get on my nerves.

The one that thinks their way is the right way and that all other theologies and methodologies are in error, Joe?

Uhh... is this the point where you whip out a mirror and hold it up to my face?

You're getting pretty good at this, Joe.

© Radio Free Babylon

Our Own Fathers

Is it true that how we view our own fathers is how we'll think of our heavenly father, Jesus?

Dads *can* affect a person's understanding of the nature and character of God, Ann. It's a huge responsibility.

Well, I'm glad *you* aren't always critical, distant, angry and drinking too much, Jesus.

Cut him some slack, Ann. And give him a call.

© Radio Free Babylon

By Design

When I walk into the house after just an hour away, my dog will greet me as if I've been gone for ten years.

By design, Lisa. It's just one of the many little pictures of God's love for you.

And when my cat just circles my legs demanding to be fed, *that's* a picture of something, I'm sure.

That's just the start of the picture, Lisa. The way your cat looks at the food and then finally, grudgingly, eats it...I could go on.

© Radio Free Babylon

Agree to Disagree

Who could forgive someone seventy times seven, Son of Man? What a *ridiculous* request! You ask your people to be walked upon!

I ask my people to forgive as they are forgiven, Satan.

Echh...whatever.
Let's just agree to disagree.

Uh...no?

The Same Mouth

Man, courtesy and decency are *disappearing* from society, Jesus! Did you see how that *stupid #@$*%&* grabbed the parking spot I was waiting for?

Whoa, Carl. Is that the same mouth you use to praise God?

This is what's known as *righteous* anger, Jesus!

I should've taught that punk a lesson.

When you're done venting, righteous one, I'm trying to teach a punk a lesson.

A Hand In It

I hope you weren't including Punkass Pilate when you said, "Father forgive them, for they know not what they do," Jesus.

It's *Pontius*, Kevin, and he was one of the least in the know as to what was going on that day.

He's the one who had you beaten bloody, mocked, cursed and finally nailed to a tree.

It was going to happen no other way, Kevin. Pilate had a hand in it.

And so do you.

The Original
COFFEE
WITH
JESUS

Custody of
The Eyes

It's just a little something from Saint Francis that I think you'd benefit from, Carl.

Yeah, thanks anyway, Padre. I don't go in for the saints stuff.

It's just a practice he advocated that I think we can all gain from.

Dude! I'm not Catholic, OK? And you're not converting me into some saint-worshiping freak show. Back off.

I'm not Catholic either, Carl.

I get that a lot. It's the collar.

Oh...sorry.

Well, and you're Hispanic, too. So, my bad, but anyway, I don't like saints.

Carl, Francis didn't ask to be called a saint. He endures because he had some great thoughts. Listen to Joe, please.

Why're you guys ganging up on me? Lisa put you both up to this, didn't she?

She didn't have to, Carl. You have a reputation around town. Anyway, Francis promoted what's called "custody of the eyes."

Look, Joe. Francis lived in the woods with a bunch of dudes. This is America in the twenty-first century, with hot chicks in tight—

A reputation? Seriously?

People think I'm some kind of perv?

You won't be held accountable for the first glance, Carl.

It's the creepy, lingering stares we're going to arrest.

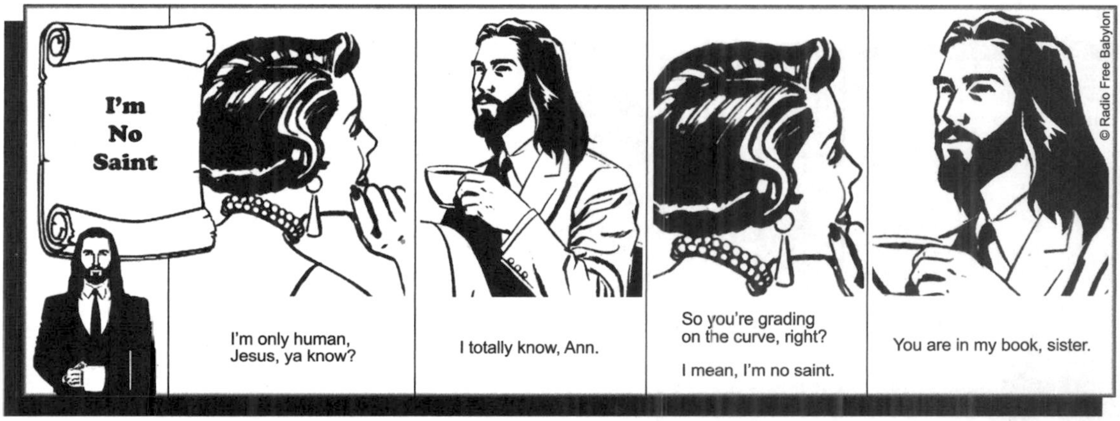
I'm No Saint
I'm only human, Jesus, ya know?
I totally know, Ann.
So you're grading on the curve, right?
I mean, I'm no saint.
You are in my book, sister.
© Radio Free Babylon

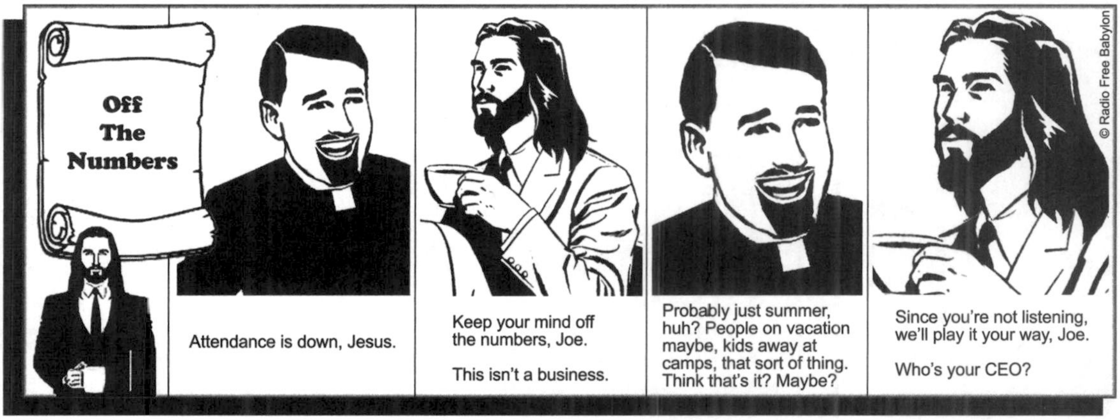
Off The Numbers
Attendance is down, Jesus.
Keep your mind off the numbers, Joe.
This isn't a business.
Probably just summer, huh? People on vacation maybe, kids away at camps, that sort of thing. Think that's it? Maybe?
Since you're not listening, we'll play it your way, Joe.
Who's your CEO?
© Radio Free Babylon

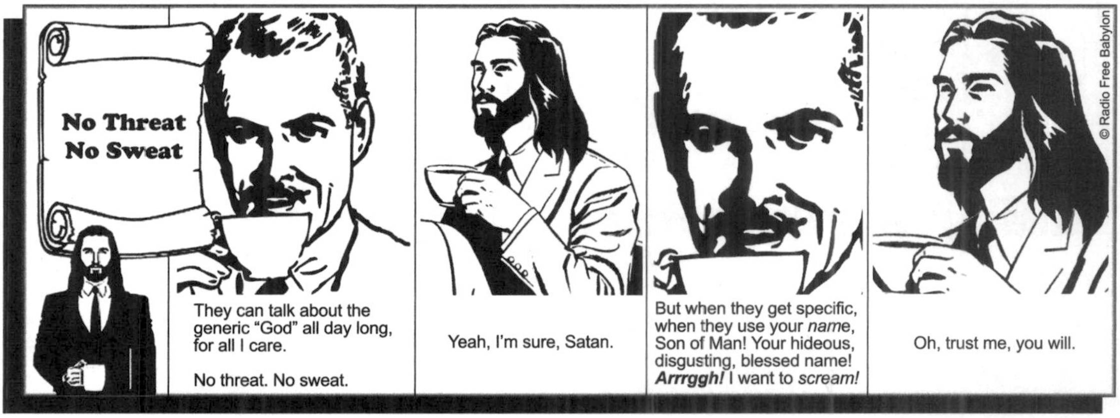
No Threat No Sweat
They can talk about the generic "God" all day long, for all I care.
No threat. No sweat.
Yeah, I'm sure, Satan.
But when they get specific, when they use your *name*, Son of Man! Your hideous, disgusting, blessed name! ***Arrrggh!*** I want to *scream!*
Oh, trust me, you will.
© Radio Free Babylon

No One's Watching

I tried to live by that saying, *"Love like you've never been hurt, dance like no one's watching,"* blah blah blah... You know that one?

Sure.

Turns out someone *was* watching...with a camera phone! And now "Idiot Dancer" on YouTube is a huge viral success.

On the plus side, Carl, you've provided encouragement to rhythmically challenged men the world over.

In Your Image

If I'm ever going to go back to church, Jesus, I'll need to find one that presents you the way *I* think of you.

You don't get to make me in your image, Kevin. I am the same Jesus today that I was yesterday; the same one I'll be forever.

And which Jesus is that? The one who talked about Hell all the time? Or the one who was full of love, mercy and compassion?

Yep.

The Other Guy

How could any person of faith even *consider* voting for him, Jesus? Absurd! His plans for this country run counter to everything you stand for!

That's exactly what they say about the other guy, Ann.

Well then, they're simply delusional! They're twisting your teachings to suit their own political agenda.

That's exactly what they say about you, Ann.

This Treadmill

Same crap, different day. This treadmill is sapping the life out of me, Jesus.

What would you change if you could, Ann?

I dunno. Maybe a job that had *meaning*? One where I was actually making some kind of *difference*?

Jobs like that are scarce. So let's start with a *difference* in attitude, Ann. Then you might even find some kind of *meaning* in this "treadmill."

© Radio Free Babylon

There but for the Grace

When I see a drunk bum on the street, Jesus, I say, "There but for the grace of God go I."

That's what you say, Carl, but what do you think?

Well, to be honest, I think, "Through bad choices and a lack of drive, that guy's getting exactly what he deserves."

I'm glad you speak before you think, Carl.

© Radio Free Babylon

You're Very Busy

Forgive me for not spending enough time with you, Jesus. I feel bad about that, but you know how hectic my schedule is, right?

You're very busy, Ann, but let's look at how much time you set aside for physical fitness every morning.

I already said I felt bad. If you're trying to make me feel guilty, then mission accomplished. Thanks.

Actually, Ann, I was trying to help you manage your time.

Ditch the earbuds and we can work out together.

© Radio Free Babylon

Nail Me Down

I know some people who worship God on Saturday, Jesus, and they think I'm wrong to worship on Sunday.

I know some people who worship God every day, Lisa.

Oh Jesus! You're doing that ambiguous, evasive thing again.

You know how I hate that!

And you, Lisa, are trying to nail me down on who's better, you or them.

You know how I hate that.

Pretty Amazing

Lisa is awesome, Jesus.

Thanks for such a wonderful woman to share my life with.

Lisa *is* pretty amazing.

She sees past all your flaws and loves you anyway, Carl.

Exactly! It's like...

Aah! *I get it!*

Nice *shot*, Jesus!

Nothin' but net, Carl.

Damage Was Done

I saw two of your people just going at it the other day, Son of Man, twisting verses this way and that to make their points, angrily arguing.

I saw the ones you speak of, Satan, and I had some words with them later.

Whatever, Boy King. The damage was done. Their "witness" to others who saw them went up in a burst of glorious flames!

Nice try, you old arsonist.

But I'm a firefighter.

Speak Their Language

Business is booming, Jesus. I just landed three more clients to my church growth consultancy.

Yay for you, Kevin. But I noted you told none of your "clients" that you're seriously doubting your faith lately.

My track record speaks for itself. I know how to get customers in the door. Plus, I can speak their language.

So maybe you could show me the same respect and refer to these "customers" as "souls," slick.

Still My Soul

Still my soul, Jesus.

I'd love to, Ann, but you'll need to work with me on this one, OK?

Whatever it takes, Jesus.

Just show me how to *slow down the racing, anxious, jangly person I've become!*

Let's start, Ann, with some practical measures, like maybe scaling back to just three cups of coffee a day instead of your usual six.

Not Qualified

I heard about this big church that's seeking a pastor, Jesus.

I'm probably not qualified, but it sure would be nice.

They're really looking for a third-degree black-belt theologian, Joe, with a collection of impressive letters behind his name.

Yeah, afraid I've never really been a part of that club. Got no books, no speaking engagements.

You're humble, Joe, good with people one-on-one, not afraid to get your hands dirty.

You are totally not qualified.

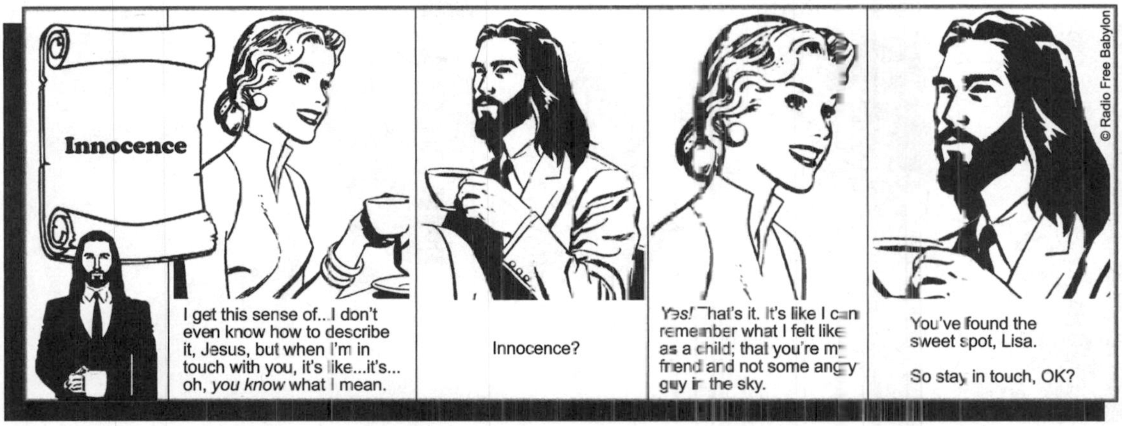
Innocence
I get this sense of...I don't even know how to describe it, Jesus, but when I'm in touch with you, it's like...it's... oh, *you know* what I mean.
Innocence?
Yes! That's it. It's like I can remember what I felt like as a child; that you're my friend and not some angry guy in the sky.
You've found the sweet spot, Lisa.
So stay in touch, OK?
© Radio Free Babylon

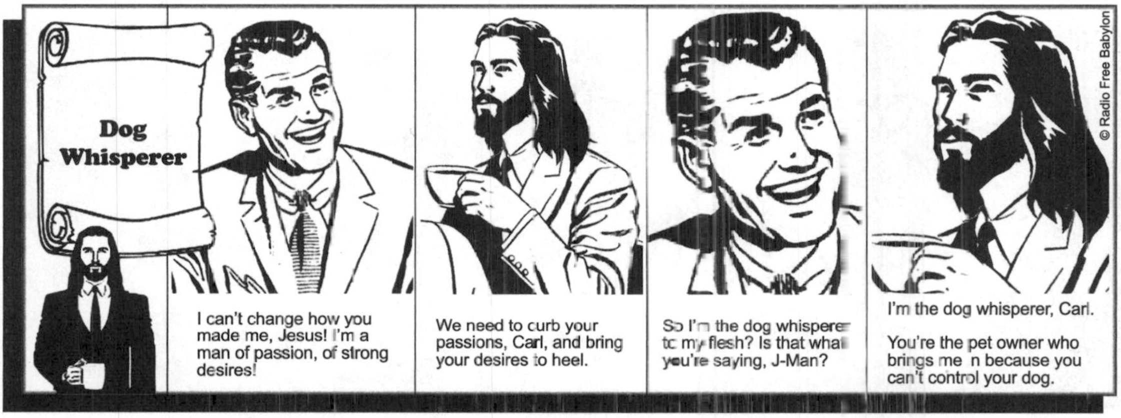
Dog Whisperer
I can't change how you made me, Jesus! I'm a man of passion, of strong desires!
We need to curb your passions, Carl, and bring your desires to heel.
So I'm the dog whisperer to my flesh? Is that what you're saying, J-Man?
I'm the dog whisperer, Carl.
You're the pet owner who brings me in because you can't control your dog.
© Radio Free Babylon

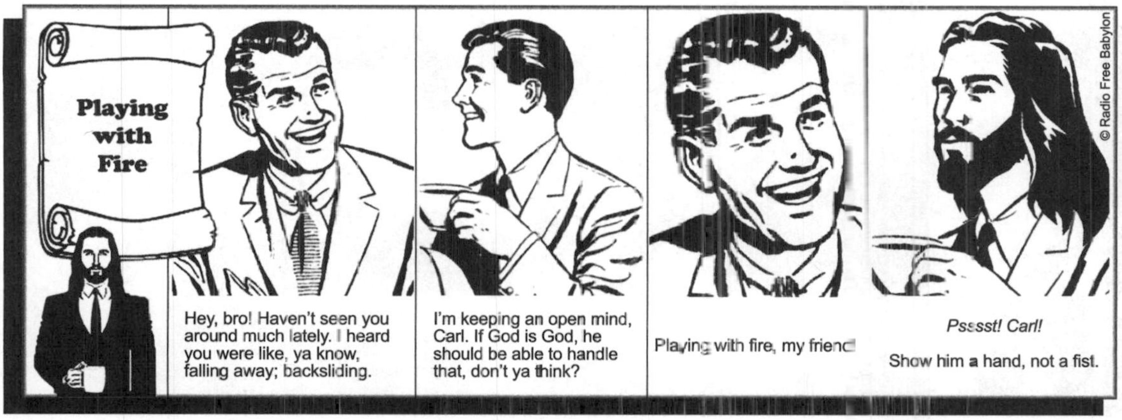
Playing with Fire
Hey, bro! Haven't seen you around much lately. I heard you were like, ya know, falling away; backsliding.
I'm keeping an open mind, Carl. If God is God, he should be able to handle that, don't ya think?
Playing with fire, my friend.
Psssst! Carl!
Show him a hand, not a fist.
© Radio Free Babylon

A Prayer

God Bless America!

Wait.
Was that a *prayer*, Ann?

*Umm...*yes?

OK. Just checking.
Kinda sounded like a demand there for a second.

Catch Myself

Sometimes I'll catch myself thinking unkind thoughts about people I don't even know, Jesus, just based on dress or hair or whatever.

That's not you catching yourself, Lisa.

I see what you mean! Because then I'll realize that I'm being judgmental and ugly and I'll try to think nicer thoughts toward them.

I like it, Lisa.
Catch ya later.

Glad Hearts

Ten percent of the congregation do ninety percent of the work, Jesus.

That ten percent do so with glad hearts, Joe.
The alternative is not very pleasant at all.

Why can't we have an entire church that helps?

We should visit your town's Walmart, Joe, where I can better illustrate for you the concept of *"Service with a Sigh."*

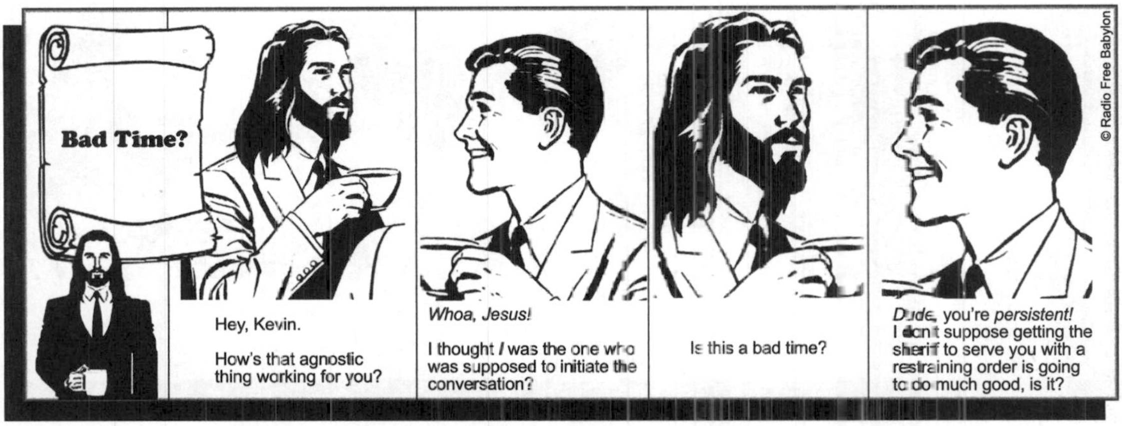
Bad Time?
Hey, Kevin.
How's that agnostic thing working for you?
Whoa, Jesus!
I thought *I* was the one who was supposed to initiate the conversation?
Is this a bad time?
Dude, you're *persistent!*
I don't suppose getting the sheriff to serve you with a restraining order is going to do much good, is it?
© Radio Free Babylon

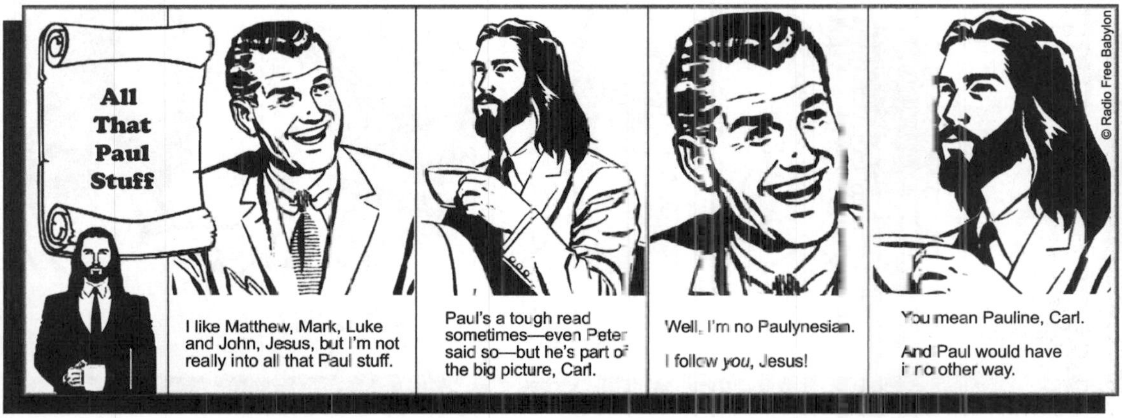
All That Paul Stuff
I like Matthew, Mark, Luke and John, Jesus, but I'm not really into all that Paul stuff.
Paul's a tough read sometimes—even Peter said so—but he's part of the big picture, Carl.
Well, I'm no Paulynesian.
I follow *you*, Jesus!
You mean Pauline, Carl.
And Paul would have it no other way.
© Radio Free Babylon

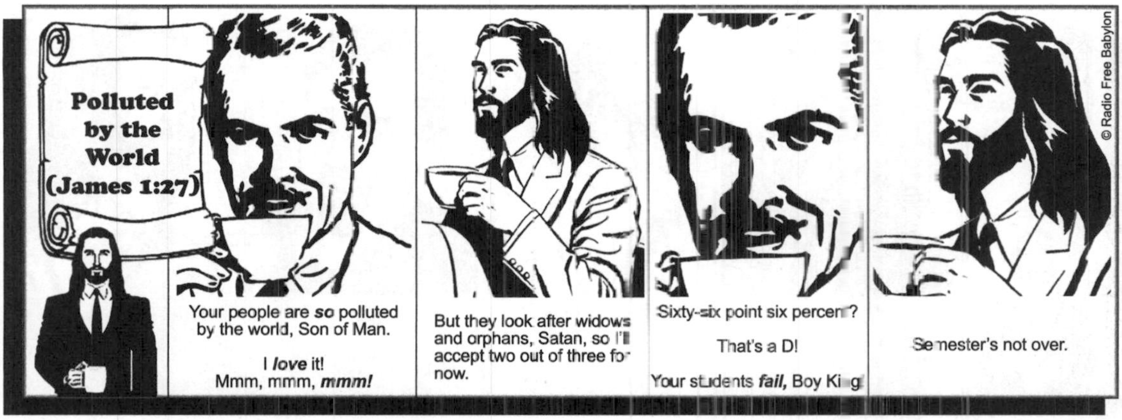
Polluted by the World (James 1:27)
Your people are *so* polluted by the world, Son of Man.
I *love* it!
Mmm, mmm, ***mmm!***
But they look after widows and orphans, Satan, so I'll accept two out of three for now.
Sixty-six point six percent?
That's a D!
Your students ***fail,*** Boy King!
Semester's not over.
© Radio Free Babylon

Bad Time? (Part II)

How long do you want to play this game of hide-and-seek, Kevin?

You're not even real! You're an imaginary friend I was tricked into believing was real a long time ago by some manipulative people!

So...*la la la la la la.*

I can't *hear* you!

You wish.

Approach God

I don't know whether to come to God in trembling fear or in familiar friendship, Jesus. Just *how* do we approach God?

When your children were young, Ann, and you picked them up from daycare, how did they approach you or their father?

They came running, arms out, smiling and shouting, "Mommy!" or "Daddy!"

That.

Better Than That

I have a lunch appointment with Pastor Steve from Worship World, Jesus. Please give me grace not to judge that strutting, conceited heretic.

I'll do better than that, Joe. I'm going to show you that the things you don't like in Steve are the very things you hate in yourself.

Oh, great.

You're going to turn us into *friends*, aren't you?

Ha!

No, Joe.

Brothers.

Fellowshipping

Carl and I are going to get together with some friends for an evening of fellowshipping, Jesus.

When did dinner and a card game become "fellowshipping," Lisa?

You're right. We should call it what it is and not try to put it into Christianese. I really feel like you've been laying this issue on my heart, Lord.

Suppose we could find another way to phrase that one, too, Lisa?

Hate Myself

It's kinda hard to love my neighbor as myself when half the time I hate myself, Jesus.

Have you noticed that you usually hate yourself, Carl, when you realize what a lover of self you are?

Wait...

You're hurting my brain.

What?

I'm saying you're making great progress.

A Total Set-Up

You knew all along that no one could measure up to your standard of holiness, so what's the point of all the commandments, Jesus?

First, to show you the standard, Kevin.

Second, to show you your need.

What I need is a really skilled criminal defense attorney to get me off of these charges. It's a total set-up—like I was framed!

Find a scapegoat, Kevin, or perhaps a compassionate advocate, maybe make your case to the well-connected son of the judge.

© Radio Free Babylon

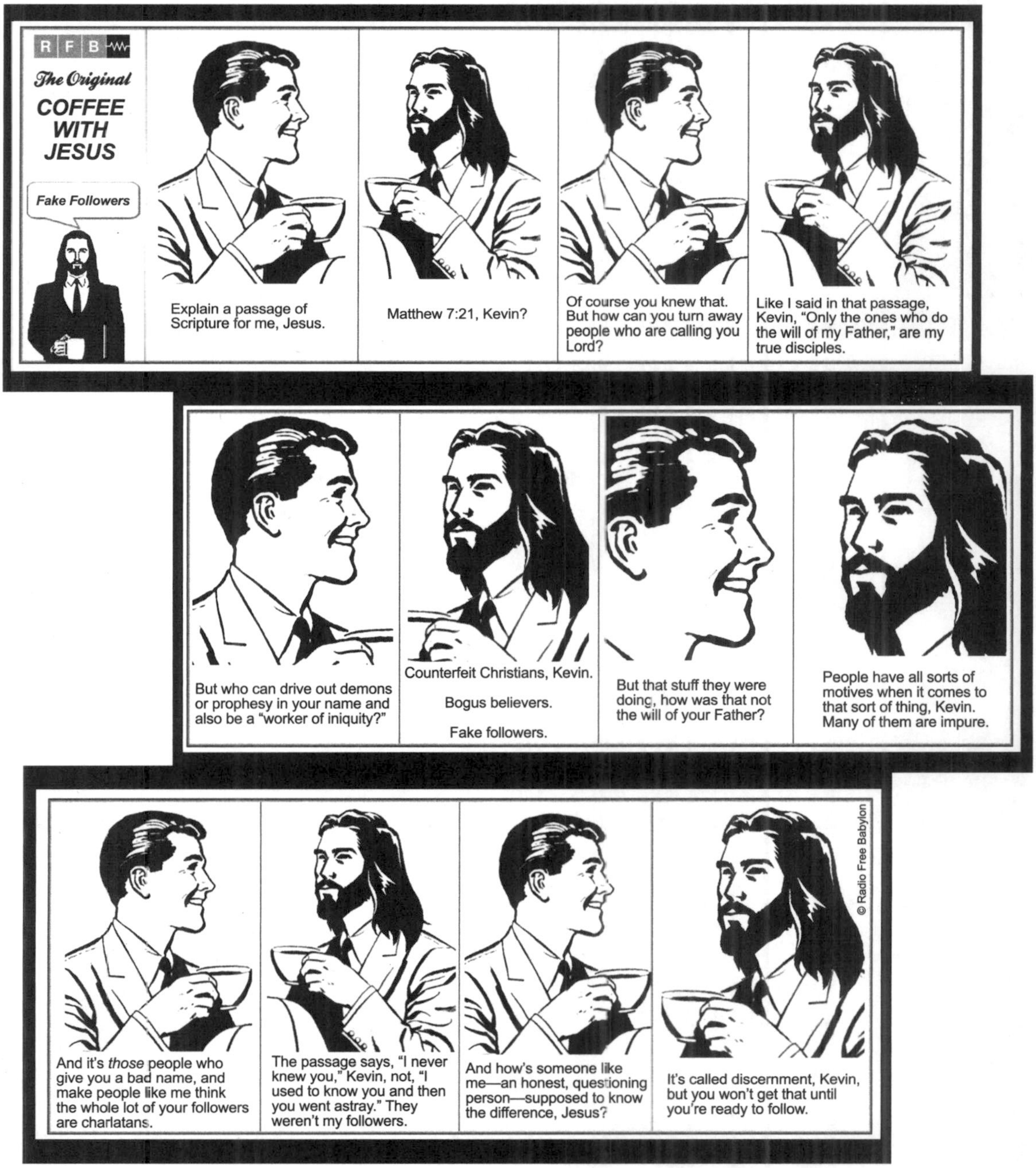
R F B
The Original
COFFEE WITH JESUS
Fake Followers
Explain a passage of Scripture for me, Jesus.
Matthew 7:21, Kevin?
Of course you knew that. But how can you turn away people who are calling you Lord?
Like I said in that passage, Kevin, "Only the ones who do the will of my Father," are my true disciples.
But who can drive out demons or prophesy in your name and also be a "worker of iniquity?"
Counterfeit Christians, Kevin.
Bogus believers.
Fake followers.
But that stuff they were doing, how was that not the will of your Father?
People have all sorts of motives when it comes to that sort of thing, Kevin. Many of them are impure.
And it's *those* people who give you a bad name, and make people like me think the whole lot of your followers are charlatans.
The passage says, "I never knew you," Kevin, not, "I used to know you and then you went astray." They weren't my followers.
And how's someone like me—an honest, questioning person—supposed to know the difference, Jesus?
It's called discernment, Kevin, but you won't get that until you're ready to follow.
© Radio Free Babylon

More Discerning

When I accuse your people of their sins, Son of Man, I have them believing they're hearing *your* voice! *So delicious!*

They're more discerning than you give them credit for, Satan.

My people know my voice.

Oh, I can mimic your voice better than your people can discern, Boy King!

Please. It's not that hard to tell the difference between a kick in the butt and a tap on the shoulder.

© Radio Free Babylon

Can't Be Christians

I see people at work, Jesus, people who I *know can't be Christians*, wearing crosses around their necks!

For many, Ann, it's nothing more than a four-leaf clover or a rabbit's foot. But how do you know they aren't Christians?

I can just tell, Jesus. They seem like party types; a little loose in the morals, if you know what I mean.

Know what you mean, Ann.

Drunkards and whores.

My kind of people.

© Radio Free Babylon

Remarkable

It's remarkable, isn't it, Jesus, that we can sit here and engage in conversation within a comic strip and no one...

I know where you're going with this, Lisa, but please, let's not offer anyone an opportunity to become incensed.

Well, I'm just trying to point out that when *our* prophet is portrayed in...

I appreciate that, Lisa, but it can come to no good.

And I'm more than a prophet, by the way.

© Radio Free Babylon

Self-Employed

Being self-employed has given me a lot of freedom, but at the same time it's forced me to be more responsible.

Joseph and I knew that story well, Carl. When you're your own boss, it's all on you.

No joke. I think the hardest part for me is I can't call in sick anymore unless I'm actually really sick.

You could still call in sick, Carl, but now you'd only be lying to yourself.

Tricky Balance

I agree with Churchill, Jesus. If you're not liberal when you're young, you have no heart. If you're not conservative when you're older, you have no brain.

Tricky balance, the heart and mind, Carl. That quote, by the way, is a legend. Churchill never said it.

Doesn't matter. It's still a great sentiment.

Not really. It implies that old people grow hard hearts and young people are brainless.

Find a balance, Carl.

Shall Not Want

The Lord is my shepherd, I shall not want...very much.

Again, Ann. From the top.

The Lord is my shepherd, I shall not... wa-...wa-... UGH! But there *is* so much that I actually *do* want, Jesus!

This might just be a King James thing, Ann. Let's try, "The Lord is my shepherd, and I have pretty much all I need" instead.

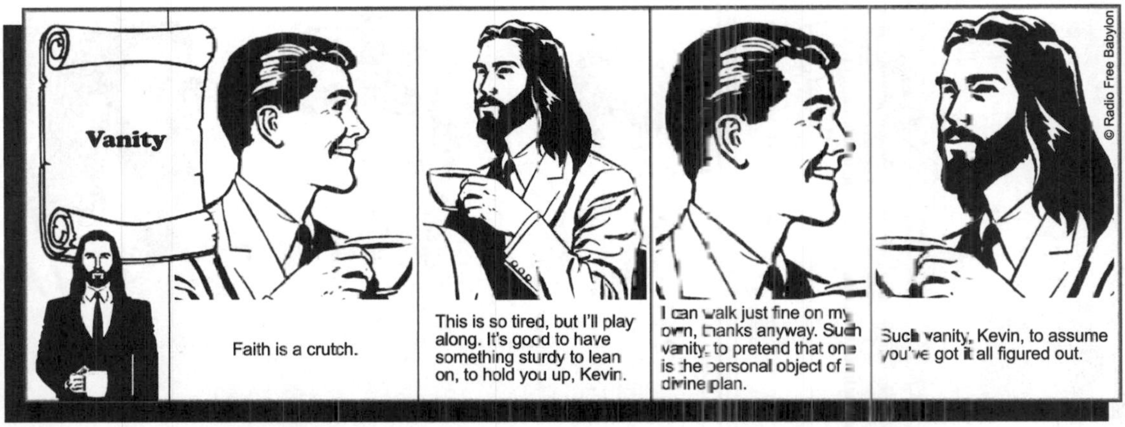
Vanity
Faith is a crutch.
This is so tired, but I'll play along. It's good to have something sturdy to lean on, to hold you up, Kevin.
I can walk just fine on my own, thanks anyway. Such vanity, to pretend that one is the personal object of a divine plan.
Such vanity, Kevin, to assume you've got it all figured out.
© Radio Free Babylon

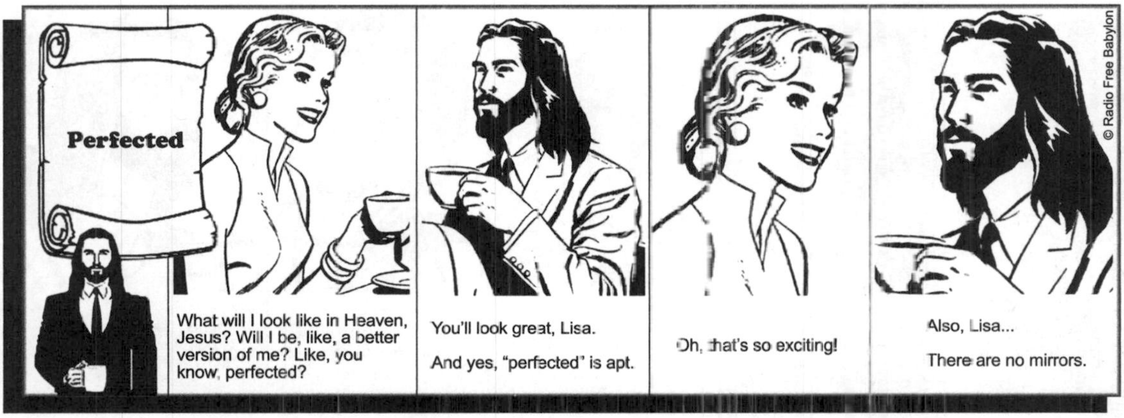
Perfected
What will I look like in Heaven, Jesus? Will I be, like, a better version of me? Like, you know, perfected?
You'll look great, Lisa.
And yes, "perfected" is apt.
Oh, that's so exciting!
Also, Lisa...
There are no mirrors.
© Radio Free Babylon

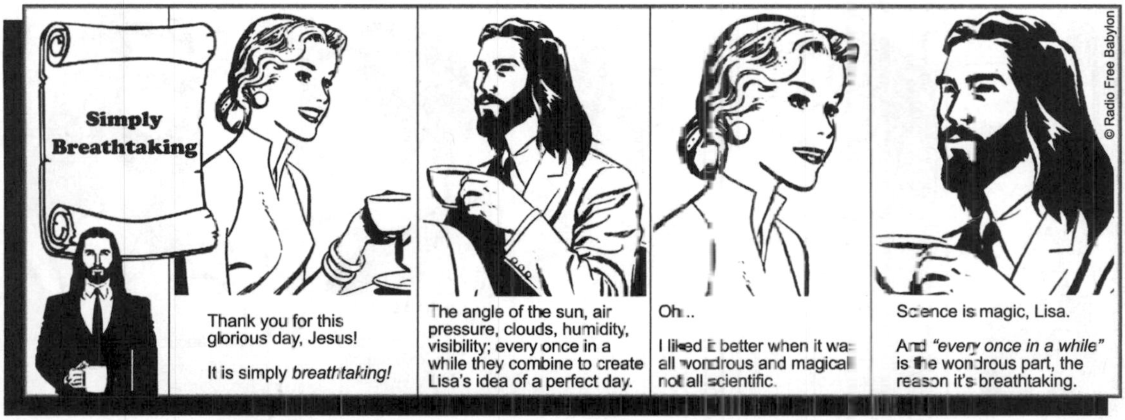
Simply Breathtaking
Thank you for this glorious day, Jesus!
It is simply *breathtaking!*
The angle of the sun, air pressure, clouds, humidity, visibility; every once in a while they combine to create Lisa's idea of a perfect day.
Oh...
I liked it better when it was all wondrous and magical, not all scientific.
Science is magic, Lisa.
And *"every once in a while"* is the wondrous part, the reason it's breathtaking.
© Radio Free Babylon

Jesus Lite™

This notion of *"Jesus is my buddy"* is a very misleading doctrine, Jesus.

I don't recommend a sort of Jesus Lite™, Lisa, but you gotta start somewhere.

People need to understand that you are *Lord*, Jesus, not their *friend!*

I'm quite fine being both, Lisa.

© Radio Free Babylon

Like and Share

I have no problem clicking the "Like" button on some of the things my friends post on Facebook, Jesus, but I sure won't share much of it.

I'm the same way, Carl.

I didn't know you were on Facebook, Jesus!

I'm not, Carl. I meant lots of people like me, but not many want to share me.

© Radio Free Babylon

Sects, Schisms and Strains

With over forty thousand sects, schisms and strains within Christianity, Jesus, is it any wonder I have my doubts about you?

Excellent point, Kevin.

But *I* haven't changed.

But *who do I listen to?*

The Roman Catholics?
The Reformers?
The Revivalists?

How about the Redeemer?

© Radio Free Babylon

Miss You Too

Sometimes the morning gets away from me, Jesus; I'll sleep in, get lost in the news online, whatever. What I'm trying to say is...

I know, Ann.

Miss you, too.

You're not disappointed that I didn't make the effort? Didn't have the discipline to spend time with you?

I don't sulk, Ann.

And I'm only a thought away.

Funny How Life Works

It's funny how all the little decisions I've made, right *and* wrong, have worked together to put me where I am now, and it's *good*.

Kinda funny how life works, isn't it, Lisa?

It's very good of you to work it all out, Jesus, although sometimes I feel like I'm taking three steps forward and then two back.

That's a net positive, Lisa!

And the important thing? You're still walking.

Total Transparency

My people think I'm *above* the daily struggles, Jesus; the same temptations *they* deal with. Anger, pride, doubt, envy, greed. I'm just a *man!*

Why do you suppose they think that way, Joe?

Are you suggesting total transparency with my congregation, Jesus?

Not suggesting at all, Joe.

Demanding.

Equal Evil Opposite

I love how I've convinced people that I'm your evil, equal opposite, Son of Man, like some sort of Darth Vader to your Obi-Wan Kenobi.

It is a shame, I'll admit, Satan, how they regard you as omniscient, omnipresent and a thing to which they should pay close attention.

I get so much credit I don't deserve! And you know what?

I'll take it!

And you know what?

I'll take it away.

Lead Us Not

What's with, "And lead us not into temptation," Jesus?

As if God would lead us into temptation?

God doesn't tempt, Carl. But do you suppose you'll face any temptations today?

Totally. It'll start with that punk competitor who needs to be taught a lesson. Then I'll probably see a few smokin' hot women. Then...

And when you don't go there, Carl, that's me, delivering you from evil.

Isn't It Awesome?

I saw a photo of Earth taken from the dark side of Saturn by a NASA probe; *900 million miles away!* And we're just this tiny blue speck, Jesus!

Yeah. Isn't it awesome?

No, Jesus! It just illustrates how *insignificant* we are!

How stupid to think we're *alone* in this vast universe!

I thought it showed *just how significant* you are, Kevin. To me, anyway.

And of course you're not alone.

© Radio Free Babylon

Day After Yesterday

I know you said we shouldn't worry about tomorrow, Jesus, but I can't *help* it. And I worry about the day *after* tomorrow! And next *week!* And next *year!*

I don't even want you to worry about the day *before* tomorrow, Ann. Or the day after yesterday.

Very funny, Jesus. You say these things like they're so easy to do.

I have *concerns!*

Go back a verse, Ann, where I told you what your *first* concern should be.

It's way less stressful that way.

Cafeteria

It's like they treat faith as a cafeteria, Jesus, picking the stuff that appeals to them and bypassing the stuff they don't like.

Meet them where they are, Joe. You don't go introducing a ribeye steak to a baby who is still nursing.

Well, at some point these babies are going to need to be weaned. And they're going to have to eat solid food.

At some point, yes, Joe.

And it will be your job to cut it into tiny little bite-sized pieces for them.

Born Again

I let myself down every day, Jesus, acting in ways I didn't want to, not doing things I wanted to do.

And you recognize it, Lisa, which is great. So forgive yourself just as I do and try to do better tomorrow, OK?

But I'm supposed to be a new creation!

I was *born again*, Jesus!

And again and again and again, Lisa.

At Least a Lieutenant

If your followers were an army, Jesus, I'd be like, what? At Least a lieutenant, right?

The first will be last and the last will be first, Carl.

That's why I'm angling to be a lieutenant, J-Man. A little authority, but not too much. It's not like I'm asking to be a general.

No, but you're asking, Carl.

So, how about we get past basic training first?

Strange Emptiness

I'm totally comfortable not believing in a god, Jesus. But late at night, staring at the ceiling, there's this... strange emptiness.

You were made for God, Kevin. That's what the emptiness is telling you.

I've come to realize that's just a crutch for weak and foolish people who refuse to face the facts, Jesus.

OK, so fill the emptiness with distractions, medications, drink and other crutches, Kevin...as you face the facts.

Beloved

I'm not worthy, Jesus.

No one is, Ann. And if you were, why am I even here?

I get that, Jesus. Still, I have a tendency to berate myself and to think that you might, too.

Ann, you are beloved.

So, please...be loved.

Hope of Mercy

The prodigal son returned to his dad driven by guilt and shame and fear of punishment, Son of Man.

Nonsense, Satan. He was driven by the hope of mercy.

Bull. You coerce and cajole, using fear and the threat of condemnation to subjugate your people, Boy King! You're a tyrant!

The father was on the porch *waiting* for him to come home, then ran to him when he saw him in the distance. Not really what I'd call arm-twisting.

Pictures of Food

I was going through pictures on my phone, Jesus, and it's just embarrassing how many times I've taken pictures of food.

Don't beat yourself up over it, Lisa. You appreciate food. Maybe taking pictures of food is just another way of being thankful for it.

You give me too much credit, Jesus. I take pictures of food to show off to my friends.

Not anymore, Lisa.

Have the Capacity

I've never been very good at Scripture memorization, Jesus. You know I've tried, but I just don't think I have the capacity.

How many lines from that funny movie you've seen a dozen times have you hidden in your heart and can recite verbatim, Carl?

Yep.

OK In My Book

Ya know, Jesus, even though I'm not a believer anymore, I still respect you. You're a good guy and a fine example. You're OK in my book.

That's nice, Kevin.

Yeah, I think I recognize that tone, Jesus.

There's a "but" coming, isn't there?

You can respect me all day long, Kevin, but that's not enough to make you OK in my book.

Tend To Tune Out

There's a couple in my congregation, Jesus, who are separating due to some, well...infidelity.

Thirty minutes of pleasure followed by thirty years of complications, Joe.

Seen it thirty million times.

Couldn't we have *stopped* it? All these damaged *lives!* Such a waste.

In these situations, Joe, people tend to tune out even the loudest of warnings.

And puppetry isn't my thing.

Another Chore

This isn't working, Jesus. I don't feel rested. I'm not at peace.

Because you've put "Spend Time with God" on a list of chores, Ann, right after "Get Kids' Breakfast" and just before "Get Ready for Work."

My day is one long list of chores, Jesus. From the moment I wake up until my head hits the pillow at night, I'm working.

And I don't want to be another chore, Ann.

How about we be coworkers?

The Lord's Prayer

Ourfatherwhoartinheavenhallowedbethynamethykingdomcomethywillbedoneonearthasitisinheavengiveusthisdayourdailybreadandforgiveus—

What are you doing, Carl?

Reciting the Lord's Prayer, Jesus.

I can hear that, Carl.

How about you try praying it instead?

Practice Praise Anyway

I'm just not feeling it, Jesus. I know we're supposed to praise you, but too often, for me anyway, it's just words.

Practice praise anyway, Ann, in private. Those words will eventually take root in your heart if you keep them on your mind.

'Il try it, Jesus, but please don't expect me to be that weirdo saying "Hallelujah" and "Praise the Lord" all day at work.

Oh, no, please don't be *that* weirdo, Ann.

Be the weirdo who says it all day in her heart.

Swinging Agnostic

I appreciate you welcoming me back a couple months ago, Jesus, but I gotta be honest, I'm swinging toward agnostic again.

You're tossed back and forth by the waves, Kevin, blown here and there by every wind of teaching and by the sleight of men.

Harsh, J-Man!

Here's the deal: *I just don't know!*

So...it's not me?

It's you?

All the More

I hope it saddens you, Son of Man, that I have turned the celebration of your birth into an orgy of wanton consumerism.

The people are all the more reminded of me, Satan, even through the fog of your deceptions.

Oh, give it a rest, Boy King! The people have barely a passing thought of you this time of year!

I can work with that.

Doom and Gloom

They're talking about all this financial doom and gloom, plus war and terrorism and crime. I'm fearful for the future, Jesus.

Do I look worried, Lisa?

Well, you never look worried, Jesus. I can always count on that.

Hello!

Move to Egypt

So what'd your parents do with the gold that the wise men from the east brought you, Jesus?

We had to move to Egypt early on, Carl, so some of it went to fund that trip. And once we got there, Joseph had to set up a new shop.

So what you're saying is that your stepdad raided your college fund!

When an angel wakes you up with, *"Get out of town, the king wants to kill your kid,"* calling your financial planner at 3 AM isn't really on your mind.

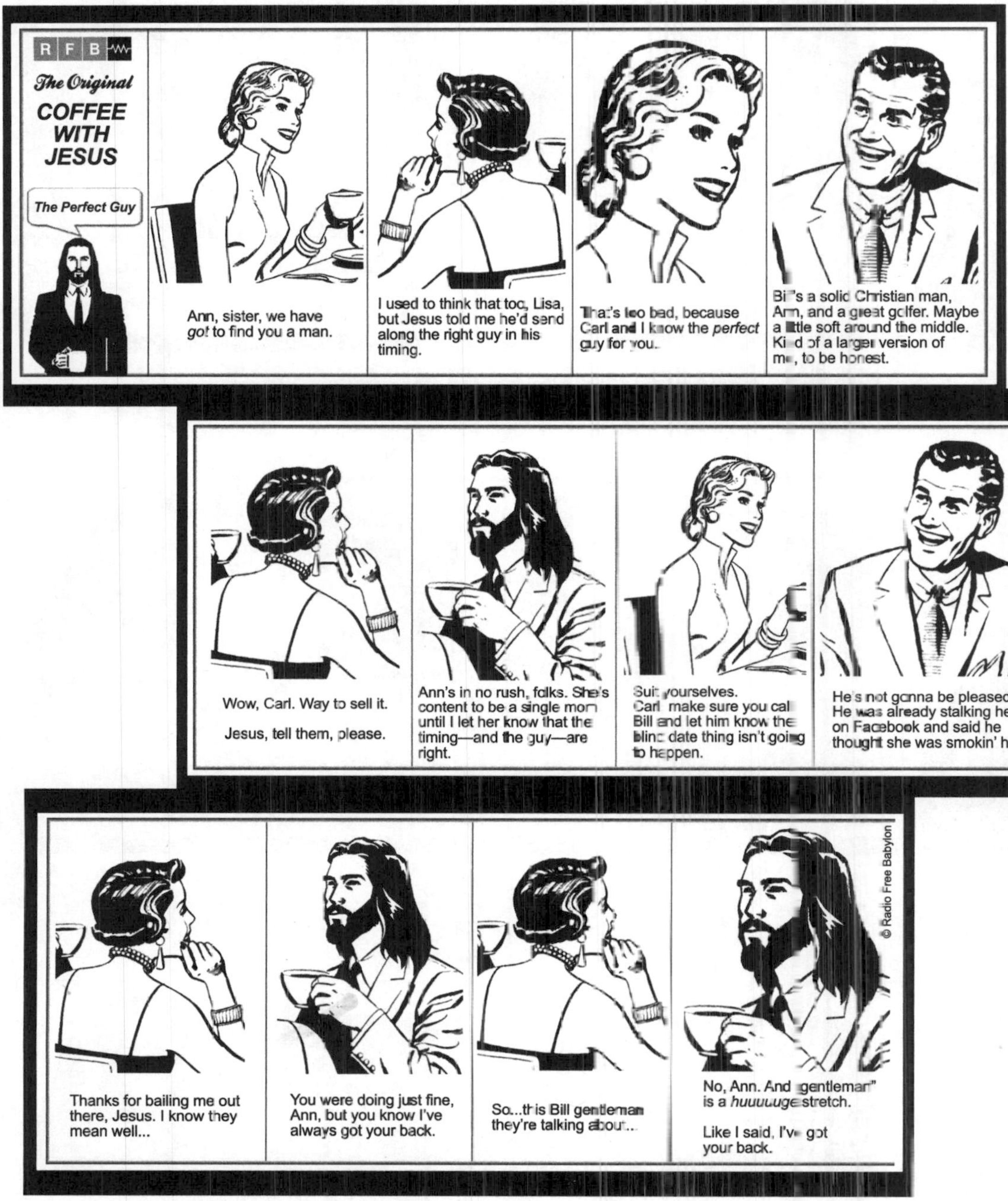
The Original
COFFEE WITH JESUS
The Perfect Guy
Ann, sister, we have *got* to find you a man.
I used to think that too, Lisa, but Jesus told me he'd send along the right guy in his timing.
That's too bad, because Carl and I know the *perfect* guy for you.
Bill's a solid Christian man, Ann, and a great golfer. Maybe a little soft around the middle. Kind of a larger version of me, to be honest.
Wow, Carl. Way to sell it.
Jesus, tell them, please.
Ann's in no rush, folks. She's content to be a single mom until I let her know that the timing—and the guy—are right.
Suit yourselves.
Carl, make sure you call Bill and let him know the blind date thing isn't going to happen.
He's not gonna be pleased. He was already stalking her on Facebook and said he thought she was smokin' hot.
Thanks for bailing me out there, Jesus. I know they mean well...
You were doing just fine, Ann, but you know I've always got your back.
So...this Bill gentleman they're talking about...
No, Ann. And "gentleman" is a *huuuuuge* stretch.
Like I said, I've got your back.
© Radio Free Babylon

Haunting Me

I thought I could shake you, Jesus, but it's like you're...

You're haunting me!

Boo!

Very funny, Jesus, but could you just let me look into some other things?

And stop harassing me!

Look all you want, Kevin, but once you go Jesus, nothing else pleases.

One Angry Dude

When I sin, Jesus, does it make you mad?

If that were the case, Ann, I'd be one angry dude pretty much all the time.

I don't *want* to sin, but it just happens, ya know?

I absolutely *do* know, Ann.

And that you don't want to is why I can't be mad at you.

Halfway There

It's so easy to *say* I forgive someone, Jesus, but the reality is I still hold bitterness toward them in my heart.

Ann, if I could bottle your honesty and distribute it...

You're halfway there!

OK, so how do I get *all the way* there?

You *say* you forgive them?

Now *pray* to forgive them.

Happy

We used to sing a song in Sunday School when I was little, Jesus. It went, *"Happy are the people whose God is the Lord."*

That comes from Psalm 144, Lisa, and I can still see you singing it; a bright-eyed, faith-filled child of God.

The thing is, I don't think I'm really happy, Jesus!

And besides, I'm not a child anymore.

A-ha!

We may have identified the problem, Lisa.

Owned

I make them think that their rituals, their works, their *pitiful efforts*, are what matter to you, Son of Man. It's a deliciously guilt-inducing concoction!

You're doing me a favor, Satan.

NEVER, Boy King!

I ruin them! I *rule* them.

I OWN them!

You're just bringing them to the end of their rope, where they realize I'm all they have.

So...owned.

One-Hour Show

I look out at the crowd, Jesus, and I wanna shout, *"Why are you here? Is this just a weekly one-hour show for you? Are your lives being transformed?"*

Do it, Joe.

Seriously, Jesus?

Absolutely, Joe. But change it to *"Why am I here? Is this just a weekly one-hour show for me? Is my life being transformed?"*

I Love You, Man

Kevin: The god myth is self-deceit. It's narcissism to the highest degree. What kind of person thinks a "creator" gives one thought to them?

Jesus: I not only think about you, Kevin, I'm concerned for you. I care about you. I'm constantly waiting for you. *I love you, man!*

Kevin: In a bro way, I trust?

Jesus: More like a father, Kevin, but if the bro thing works for you, we'll go with that.

Home Inspection

Ann: If you were to do a home inspection, so to speak, of my life, Jesus, how would you grade it?

Jesus: Hard to say, Ann. Will I have access to the closets, alcoves, the attic and all the other sealed-off spaces where I'm not welcome?

Ann: It's not that you're not welcome, Jesus, it's just that...*ummm*, well...those areas aren't ready for you.

Jesus: So before I do the home inspection, Ann, maybe you invite me in to do the repair and cleaning first?

Further Along

Carl: I'm such a screw-up, Jesus.

Bad husband, lousy father, crappy friend. I'm always falling short.

Jesus: Go a little easier on yourself, Carl. Did you think you'd be perfect by this point?

Carl: Well, not perfect, Jesus, but much further along than I am!

Jesus: Ya know, Carl from five years ago would've never given these things a second thought.

Knock on Wood

I forgot to put on my gold cross necklace this morning, Jesus! I feel so vulnerable and unprotected without it!

The cross isn't a good luck charm. This isn't superstition, Lisa. Are bad things going to befall you because you forgot your expensive little cross?

Oh, I pray not!

Knock on wood.

Nah...

Do one or the other.

Please You

I know I don't always please you, Jesus.

But you want to, Ann.

Of course, Jesus, but that...

That pleases me, Ann.

Eyes Off of Me

You know what I think finally did it for me, Jesus, as far as why I didn't need your brand of religion anymore?

Yes I do, Kevin. You got your eyes off of me and started fixating on the people who claim to be my followers.

Oh, why can't you just own your mistakes, Jesus! You allowed a bunch of proud, mean, judgment-filled haters to represent you!

It wasn't a mistake to open the door to everyone, Kevin; even the proud, mean, judgment-filled haters of the proud, mean, judgment-filled haters.

Long Game

Whiter teeth, firmer abs, silkier hair, smoother skin.

This is *so easy*, Son of Man!

The people figure you out eventually, Satan.

And once they've bought *that* lie, I sell them sleep aids, antidepressants and self-help books! God, I *love* this game!

I'm more of a long game guy.

And you're playing right into my hands.

Practicing

I meet people in town who claim to follow you, Jesus, but they aren't what I'd call "practicing" Christians.

Yeah, Joe, a lot of people have been turned off by formal religion, but don't count them out.

I think they need to be involved in a local church, Jesus, not "forsaking the assembling," ya know?

Who says they are?

Two or more, Joe.

Creature of Habit

Hey, J-Man. Sorry I didn't wake up and have my usual time with you the last couple of days. Been runnin' late.

Don't sweat it, Carl. But you know, there's a lot of time during the day when we could hang out.

I know, Jesus, but I have a routine that I don't like to deviate from. I'm a creature of habit. You understand!

I understand Rush Limbaugh and Sean Hannity both get three hours with you every day and I get a "Hi!" and "Bye!" if you wake up in time.

Figured Out

I grew up believing in you, but the more I study, the more I pray, the *less I know*, if that makes sense, Jesus.

Makes total sense, Lisa. It sounds like you're not so certain about some things anymore. You don't have me quite "figured out."

Yes! Its like what I was so certain of isn't so certain anymore and then I'm like...

I'm like...I totally *need* you!

I live for days like this, Lisa.

Will Work Out

The preacher said all I had to do was believe and that God would begin to move, to change my circumstances and make me successful.

That's some nice stuff for itching ears, Ann. But if things don't work out as you believe they will, what then?

Oh, but they *will* work out, Jesus!

I *believe* they will, and so they will.

Lord willing.

Sort of Zen

That whole "take no thought for tomorrow" business is a really crappy retirement plan, Jesus.

I never said don't save money or don't plan for the future, Kevin. I was saying today should be your focus, not tomorrow or yesterday.

I suppose I could get behind that concept.

It's sort of Zen, which is cool.

No, Kevin. It's pure Jesus.

Way cooler.

Moments In Days

There are times, Lisa, when I could swear you don't like me very much.

There are days, Carl, or rather, moments in days, when you can be quite a challenge. I'm sure you'd say the same about me.

You can frustrate the hell out of me, Lisa, but love, I've heard it said, isn't a feeling. It's an action. So, I'm gonna keep loving you.

Get a room, you two.

No, seriously.

© Radio Free Babylon

Seen by Others

Some local pastors want me to join them for their "Pray for Our Nation" rally next week at the county courthouse, Jesus.

How nice, Joe. Everyone gathered to pray on street corners to be seen by others. I trust all the local news outlets will be there?

Oh, come on, Jesus! I've been invited to this thing! Am I supposed to tell these people, "Sorry, I'm too good for your event"?

No, Joe. Tell them you'll join them...in Spirit.

In private.

© Radio Free Babylon

Let It Go

Sometimes, Jesus, I'll be reminded of stuff I did years ago, stuff I'm ashamed of, stuff I *confessed* to you, and I'll get this fresh sense of guilt.

I keep no record of wrongs, Carl, so it isn't me doing the reminding.

So, that time in college, when me and the guys went off and did that thing...

You know...

Actually, no, I don't, Carl.

Let it go. I did.

© Radio Free Babylon

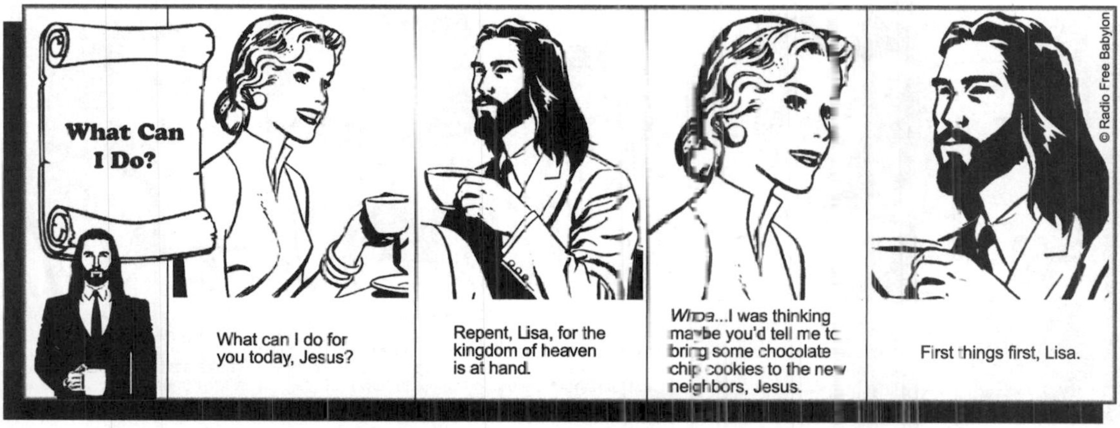
What Can I Do?
What can I do for you today, Jesus?
Repent, Lisa, for the kingdom of heaven is at hand.
Whoa...I was thinking maybe you'd tell me to bring some chocolate chip cookies to the new neighbors, Jesus.
First things first, Lisa.
© Radio Free Babylon

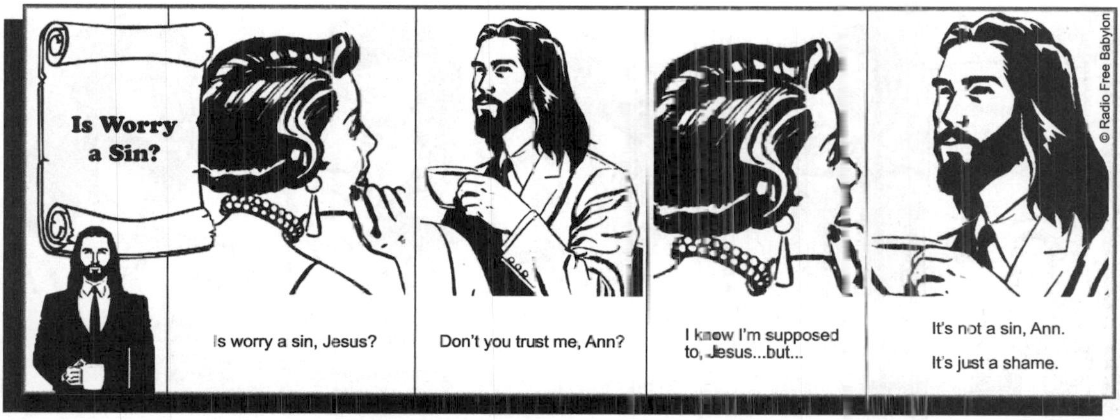
Is Worry a Sin?
Is worry a sin, Jesus?
Don't you trust me, Ann?
I know I'm supposed to, Jesus...but...
It's not a sin, Ann.
It's just a shame.
© Radio Free Babylon

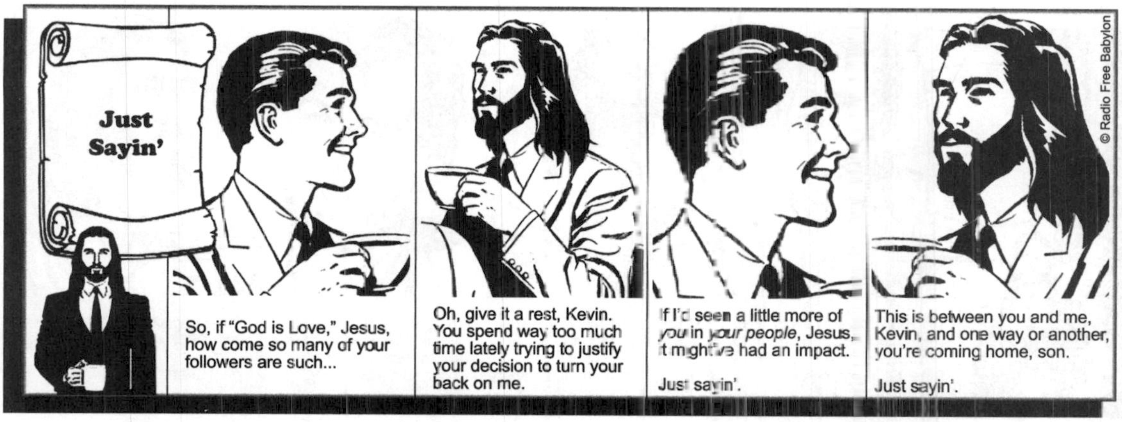
Just Sayin'
So, if "God is Love," Jesus, how come so many of your followers are such...
Oh, give it a rest, Kevin. You spend way too much time lately trying to justify your decision to turn your back on me.
If I'd seen a little more of *you* in *your people*, Jesus, it might've had an impact.
Just sayin'.
This is between you and me, Kevin, and one way or another, you're coming home, son.
Just sayin'.
© Radio Free Babylon

Many in This Place

Look at this country, Son of Man! "In God We Trust," they say. "One Nation Under God," they say. I *laugh!* They trust everything *but* you!

I have many in this place who are real, Satan. They delight in me and I in them.

You can't take that from us.

Oh, please, Boy King! *Delight* in you? They use you as a hammer to judge their fellows! You are their license to *hate!*

The loud and the proud have no place with me, Satan.

You're confusing my children with your own.

Same Old Apologies

Sorry about yesterday, Jesus.

I'll try to do better today.

We cool?

Every day's a new day.

I'm here for you, Carl.

We're cool.

Don't you ever get sick of this, Jesus? Me and my same old screw-ups and my same old apologies?

Two-way street, Carl.

Do you ever get sick of my same old forgiveness?

World to Come

Do you think you could give me a near death experience, Jesus, and then I could write a best-selling book about it?

Plenty of those books out there already, Carl.

So, no, not going to happen.

But people need hope, Jesus. They want to hear about heaven and the world to come.

"I go to prepare a place for you" was packed with hope.

You heard it here first.

Hearts of Fire

What do my people need most, Jesus?

Hearts of fire, Joe.

Oh. I thought you'd say something like "deeper faith," or "love for their neighbor," or maybe just "compassion."

You're describing the qualities of people with hearts of fire, Joe.

Mini-Lent

My church doesn't do the whole "give something up for Lent" thing, Jesus, but I kinda want to try it. Is it too late?

Easter is still weeks away, Ann. You can start your own mini-Lent.

OK. What should I give up?

Procrastinating?

Something Better

I saw a "Christian" film last night, Jesus. Bad writing, bad directing, bad acting. It was just laughable.

Can you create something better, Kevin?

It wouldn't take much!

Selling to a Christian audience is easy.

Then your answer is no.

Attitudes like that are exactly why the film you watched was laughable.

— 65 —

Sick Day

I'm taking a sick day today, Jesus. Gonna enjoy an extended weekend.

You should've taken a personal day since you aren't really sick, Ann.

I know, I know. But I already called my boss and did the pretend sick voice, Jesus.

Yeah, that's too bad, Ann, because come Monday the lies continue when you pretend to be all better.

Got This Covered

In the end, Jesus, I mean, if there really *is* a God, he's going to look at my life and see that the good things I did outweighed the bad.

So you're telling me you don't need me anymore, Kevin. You've got this covered, is that it?

I like the freedom I have now, Jesus. I'm no longer shackled by constant guilt, fear and worry that I'm not pleasing "the man upstairs."

Shackled...? Guilt, fear and worry...?

You're doing it wrong, Kevin

Even the Devil

I can get the measure of a man just by his handshake. It's a gift I have. Kinda just size him up in a matter of seconds.

Even the devil will look you in the eye and offer a firm handshake, Carl.

I'm not so easily fooled, Jesus. I can spot a swindler or a cheat a mile away.

Said the former timeshare salesman.

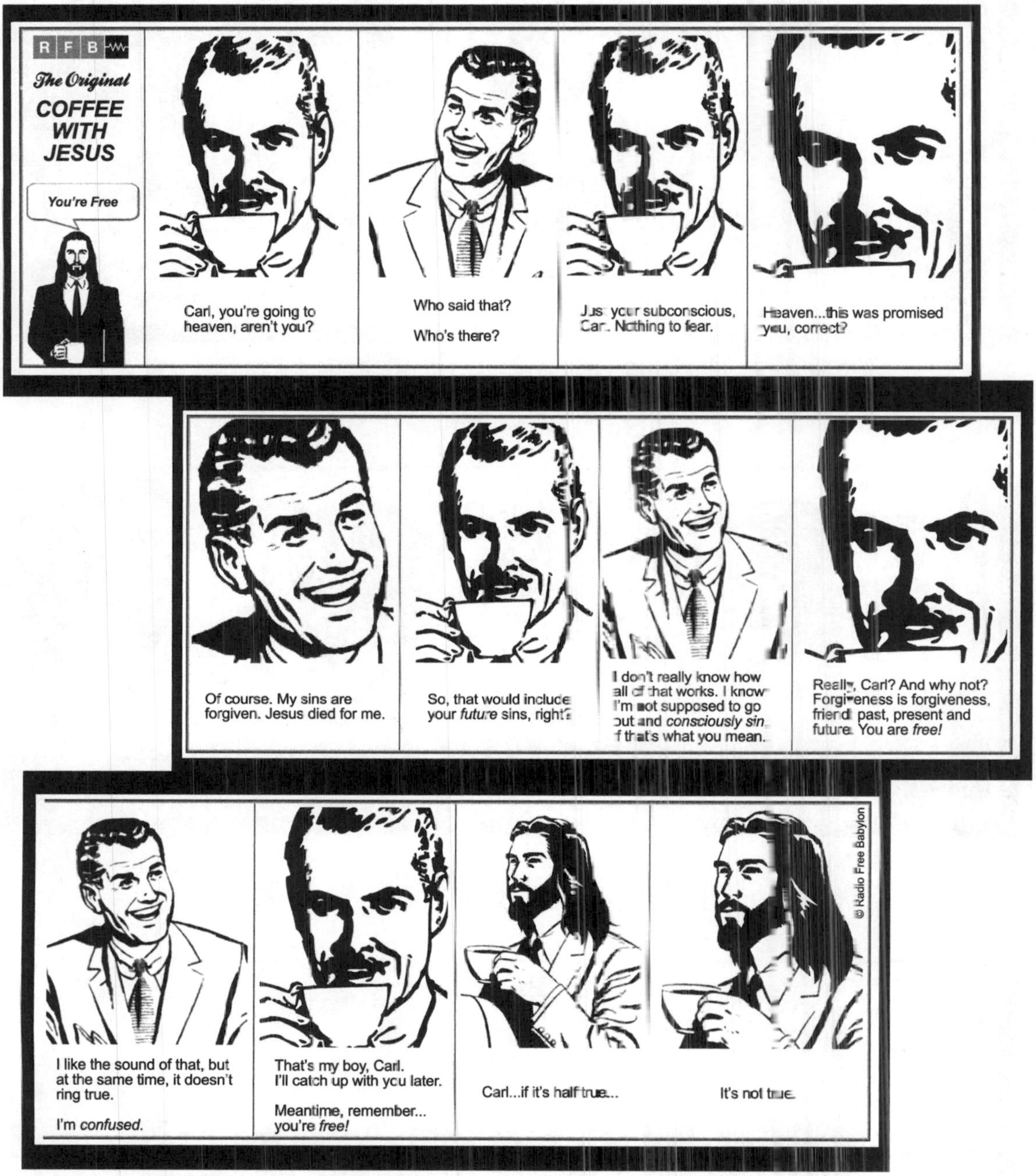
RFB
The Original
COFFEE WITH JESUS
You're Free
Carl, you're going to heaven, aren't you?
Who said that?
Who's there?
Just your subconscious, Carl. Nothing to fear.
Heaven...this was promised you, correct?
Of course. My sins are forgiven. Jesus died for me.
So, that would include your *future* sins, right?
I don't really know how all of that works. I know I'm not supposed to go out and *consciously sin*, if that's what you mean.
Really, Carl? And why not? Forgiveness is forgiveness, friend: past, present and future. You are *free!*
I like the sound of that, but at the same time, it doesn't ring true.
I'm *confused*.
That's my boy, Carl.
I'll catch up with you later.
Meantime, remember... you're *free!*
Carl...if it's half true...
It's not true.
© Radio Free Babylon

I'm Not Your Genie

I'm not seeing any results from my prayers, Jesus.

That's because you're thinking of "results" as *stuff*, Lisa; things you want. I'm not your genie!

OK, then.

Help me to not want stuff!

Now, *that's* a prayer that's going to produce some real results, Lisa.

No Probably About It

I probably don't read the Bible as much as I should, Jesus.

There's no probably about it, Ann. If I hid all your Bibles, even the two on your phone, I don't think you'd notice they were gone.

Oh, I'd definitely notice if the Bible in my living room went missing, Jesus.

The giant, decorative one?

Of course.

The Wrong Direction

I have a pretty good sense of which way my congregation leans politically, Jesus, and it's not *my* way.

And I didn't call you to lead a political movement, Joe.

Your job is to shepherd.

I get that, Jesus. So how do I stand by and watch as these sheep run off in the wrong direction?

You encourage them to pray for their leaders; as earnestly for the other side as for their own. And the *only* kingdom you endorse, Joe, is mine.

Reasonable

La la la la la laaaa...

Hmmmm, hmmmm, hmm...

Pretending I'm not here won't make me disappear, Kevin.

di∂n't hear that! My m nd s jus' playing tricks on me! Sure y there's a scientilic, reasonable explanation for this.

I *created* science, Kevin.

So come, let us reason.

Denying the Power

Things are great right now, Son of Man. So many traitors, heady, highminded, lovers of pleasure more than lovers of God.

Depending on where you hang out, those people have always been easy to find, Satan.

Oh, I've found them! *Love* these pretenders, having a form of godliness, but denying the power thereof!

You can even quote the Bible like they do.

Washington suits you quite well, doesn't it?

A Little Harder

I'm so glad you gave me a Christian husband, Jesus. Carl was saved in like, fourth grade or whatever. That's so great, Jesus.

Yep. Vacation Bible School at a tiny Baptist church in Texas. Remember it well.

Good times.

Yeah...that's awesome Jesus. But couldn't you have saved him maybe... a little *harder*? He just doesn't burn very brigh

He burns just fine, Lisa.

How about you toss that log in your eye onto your own fire?

Nothing Can Separate You

You love me, I know, Jesus.

I mean, that's said over and over again in the Bible.

Sure enough, Ann.

Nothing can separate you from that.

That's so reassuring, Jesus.

But...do you *like* me?

If the Book of Life had a "thumbs-up" icon next to your name, Ann...I would click that thing a billion times.

Rockin' the Boat

This new Pope, Jesus, he's really making some waves.

He's rockin' the boat, that's for sure, Carl.

I kinda like the guy!

And I'm not even Catholic!

Me too, Carl.

And neither am I.

I Have This Against You

My denomination is simply *contending for the faith*, Jesus! We don't want to see it watered down, taken lightly, misrepresented or perverted!

I admire that zeal, Joe. You search the Scriptures. Awesome. Keep it up.

But I have this against you...

Crap. I *hate* it when you say that.

But go ahead.

Contend, but don't condescend, condemn, congratulate yourself and become conceited. Pride is ugly, Joe. But spiritual pride is, well...like super ugly.

Legitimate to Me

My "conversion" wasn't even real, Jesus, if you think about it. Boy chases girl to youth group? Gets "saved"? How can that be legitimate?

I've thought about it, Kevin. It was legitimate to me.

You can recall the reality, the joy of that encounter.

Nah...it was emotion and coercion. So many of your followers "find you" as kids. They're not thinking, easily swayed—it's peer pressure.

They *do* find me, Kevin. And then many—not mentioning any names—spend the rest of their lives trying to convince themselves they never did.

Selfies Everywhere

The camera phone has been the biggest boost to vanity since the mirror, Son of Man! Selfies everywhere, all the time! *Love* it!

Well before the mirror, the created were taking pride in their beauty, Satan.

Need I remind you...

NO! You need *not!*

<*sniff*>

I was *soooo* beautiful....

Wow.

You should see yourself right now.

Two-Faced

I catch myself throughout the day judging others, putting myself above people, and just being an ugly, ugly person, Jesus!

And yet the Lisa I talk to every morning is humble, innocent, open and sweet.

What's up with that?

Are you saying I'm two-faced, Jesus?

Kinda sorta, Lisa, but it goes a little deeper than that. It's called double-minded. So, the face you show me? Try showing it to everyone else.

Faithful and True

I was reading Revelation again, Jesus, and you are *scary!* A sword coming out of your mouth, robe dipped in blood, riding a white horse!

Some find that imagery a little graphic, Ann, but what does John say the one riding the horse is called?

"...And he that sat upon him was called Faithful and True."

See? How scary is that?

And thanks for not calling it "Revelations" this time.

© Radio Free Babylon

Spirit Animal

If I believed in this sort of stuff, Jesus—and of course I don't—I think my spirit animal would be a wolf. Or an eagle!

If that sort of stuff were real, Carl, there'd be way too many wolves and eagles. Nobody ever says loon. Or ox. Or jackass.

OK, maybe I'd be a snow leopard! Or, *no!* A *wild stallion!* Yeah, *that's* me!

Whoa there, big fella.

I'd be a lamb. Or a lion.

Or both.

© Radio Free Babylon

Happy Fun Stuff

Last Sunday's sermon did NOT go over well, Jesus. I might've stepped on some toes. Might've even kicked a few heads, I'm afraid.

How're we ever gonna grow this church, Joe? The people want happy fun stuff! You can't go making them all uncomfortable like that!

I didn't think it was my job to give them happy fun stuff, Jesus. I tried to speak the truth in love. I'm sorry if I made them uncomfortable.

Just playin' with ya, Joe! You were a *ninja* up there! Sacred cows flying every which way!

In love, of course.

© Radio Free Babylon

The Jesus I Like

You had some wise sayings, Jesus, like "Do unto others," and "Judge not." That's the Jesus I like. Knowledge without all the other junk.

"The fear of the Lord is the beginning of knowledge," Kevin...

You lost me already with the God-talk, Jesus. I'm looking for the *Wisdom of the Great Masters* type of stuff. Make it more Confucius-y.

And you only heard half of it, Kevin.

"...but fools despise wisdom and instruction."

Gold Nuggets

Unlike me, Son of Man, you can see into *the secrets of their souls!* That must be so *deliciously depressing* for you! All that filfth!

I seek the gold nuggets, Satan. And sifting past the rubbish, I can usually find them.

Oh, how sweet!

And what happens when you *don't find them*, Boy King?

Then I plant them there.

Fall Asleep Praying

Sometimes—well, actually, a lot of times, Jesus—I'll fall asleep while I'm praying.

When your child dozes off in your lap, Lisa, do you shake her awake? 'Course not.

Sweetest thing ever, right?

But you scolded your disciples when they fell asleep in the garden.

If your child dozes off in your lap while your house is on fire, Lisa, do you shake her awake?

Context, girl.

Do the Hard Thing

She's out to get me, Jesus! We've never been able to get along and it just gets worse every day. *GOD*, I *can't stand* that woman!

I appreciate your honesty, Ann.

Now, do the hard thing.

Fine...Jesus, please turn that wicked woman around and change her into someone who isn't such a pain in the ass. Amen.

OK, this is gonna take some work, Ann.

But great start.

Here We All Are

What if my dad had never met my mom, or *their parents* hadn't met each other! And *their parents!* And *on and on and on*, all the way back!

Or what if David hadn't met Bathsheba! Or Ruth hadn't met Boaz! And on and on and on, all the way back, Carl.

So it's like you can keep it all straight and make it work, despite our bad choices and missteps.

Here we all are, Carl.

Nothing's an accident.

The Sower

So, Jesus, some seed falls on the path, some seed falls on the rocks. Some seed among the thorns and some in the good soil, right?

Before you pick apart one of my favorite parables, Joe, keep in mind that agricultural technology was still pretty primitive in the first century.

Still, this is one wasteful seed-spreader we're dealing with here, isn't it? Just tossing seeds all over the place willy-nilly?

I'd rather cover the whole place than miss a spot, Joe.

And it's not like I'll be running out of seed.

Talking to Myself

I'm not some anomaly, Jesus. Look around! People are leaving the faith in droves. They're done with the game. They're wising up!

How is it, Kevin, that in your new agnosticism, you come to me daily to justify it?

Habit, I suppose. Really, I'm just talking to myself.

Right?

I'll let you answer that.

Cries

Wanna hear my impression of your followers, Son of Man?

No, I really don't, Satan

Well, here it is anyway:

"Gimme, gimme, gimme! Bless, bless, bless! Waaa! Waaa! Waaa!"

Not that you'd understand this, but one never hears the cries of another's child quite like the parent does.

I'm not Stupid

You know my type, Jesus. I'm a take-charge guy. Can't be "waiting on the Lord," as they say. No offense, but I like to take matters into my own hands.

I understand that desire to solve things, Kevin, but you rush headlong into trouble if you lack wisdom.

Experience is a great teacher, Jesus. I'm not stupid, you know.

But nor are you wise.

Salt and Light

You told your people to be salt and light, Son of Man, but look at them.

Your opinions of my people, Satan, are suspect by nature.

I bring you *facts*, Boy King! They are not salt! Neither are they light! What excuse can you make for them? They stand *accused!*

They stand pardoned, Satan.

The Right Path

Is it possible, Jesus, for someone to *think* they're on the right path, but they're totally not? Like, they're way off?

Very possible, Lisa. I could name for you hundreds of sects that have gone off the path, straying into error.

Oh, my. That's so sad.

How does that happen?

Easy, Lisa. They follow their leader...who isn't following me.

Not Feeling It

Not feeling it today, Jesus.

Not one bit. Sorry.

Yeah, I know, Ann.

So, aren't you gonna snap me out of it? Make me not be this way?

That's what drugs do, Ann.

I'd rather walk you through it than snap you out of it.

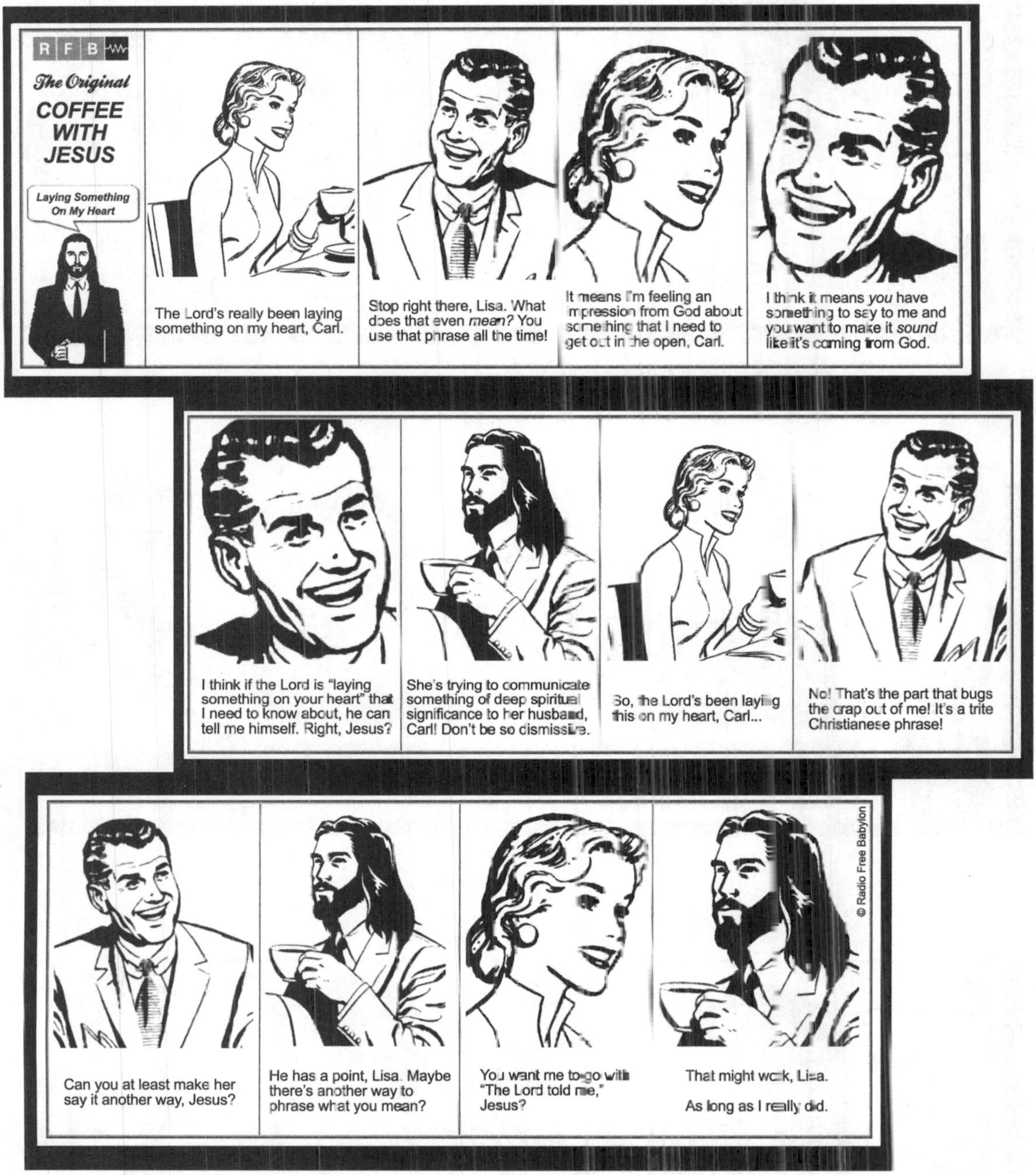
R F B
The Original
COFFEE WITH JESUS
Laying Something On My Heart
The Lord's really been laying something on my heart, Carl.
Stop right there, Lisa. What does that even *mean?* You use that phrase all the time!
It means I'm feeling an impression from God about something that I need to get out in the open, Carl.
I think it means *you* have something to say to me and you want to make it *sound* like it's coming from God.
I think if the Lord is "laying something on your heart" that I need to know about, he can tell me himself. Right, Jesus?
She's trying to communicate something of deep spiritual significance to her husband, Carl! Don't be so dismissive.
So, the Lord's been laying this on my heart, Carl...
No! That's the part that bugs the crap out of me! It's a trite Christianese phrase!
Can you at least make her say it another way, Jesus?
He has a point, Lisa. Maybe there's another way to phrase what you mean?
You want me to go with "The Lord told me," Jesus?
That might work, Lisa.
As long as I really did.
© Radio Free Babylon

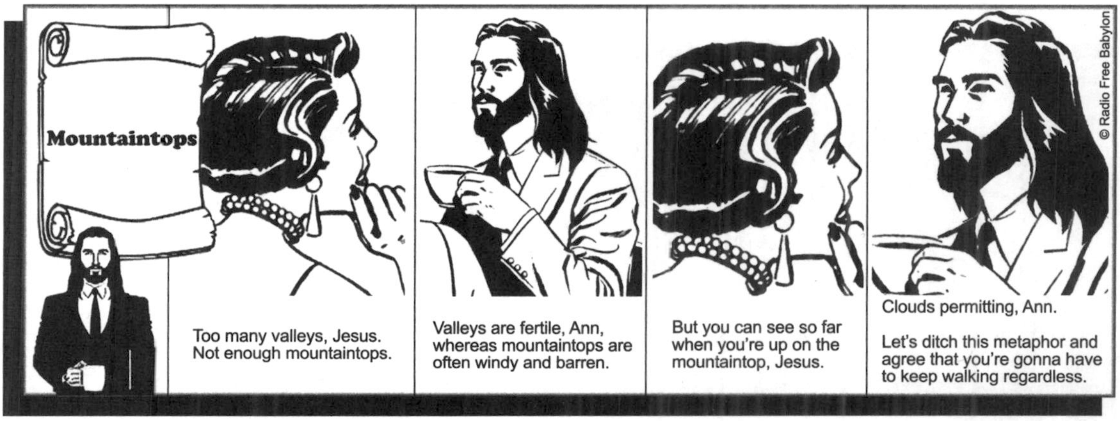
Mountaintops
Too many valleys, Jesus. Not enough mountaintops.
Valleys are fertile, Ann, whereas mountaintops are often windy and barren.
But you can see so far when you're up on the mountaintop, Jesus.
Clouds permitting, Ann.
Let's ditch this metaphor and agree that you're gonna have to keep walking regardless.
© Radio Free Babylon

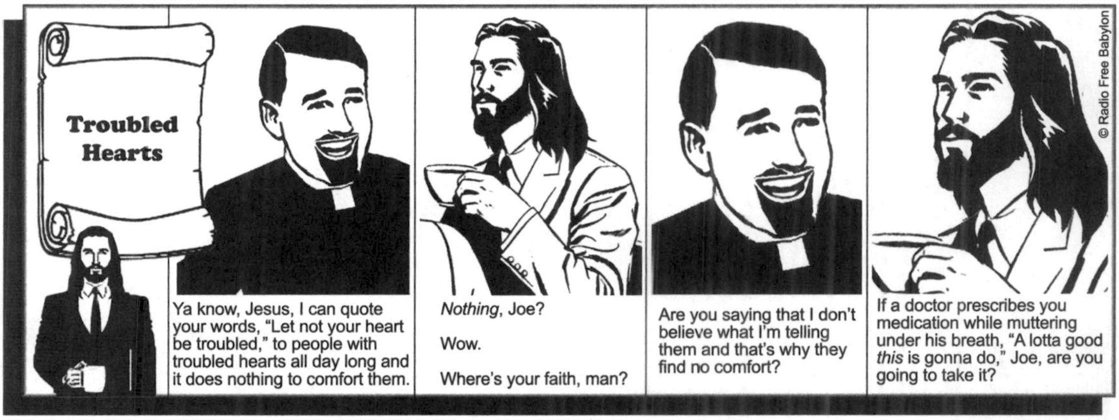
Troubled Hearts
Ya know, Jesus, I can quote your words, "Let not your heart be troubled," to people with troubled hearts all day long and it does nothing to comfort them.
Nothing, Joe?
Wow.
Where's your faith, man?
Are you saying that I don't believe what I'm telling them and that's why they find no comfort?
If a doctor prescribes you medication while muttering under his breath, "A lotta good *this* is gonna do," Joe, are you going to take it?
© Radio Free Babylon

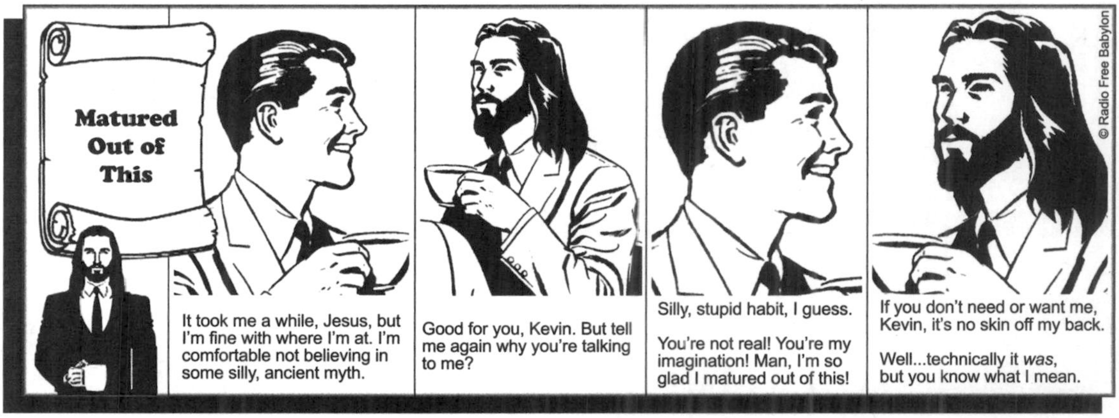
Matured Out of This
It took me a while, Jesus, but I'm fine with where I'm at. I'm comfortable not believing in some silly, ancient myth.
Good for you, Kevin. But tell me again why you're talking to me?
Silly, stupid habit, I guess.
You're not real! You're my imagination! Man, I'm so glad I matured out of this!
If you don't need or want me, Kevin, it's no skin off my back.
Well...technically it *was*, but you know what I mean.
© Radio Free Babylon

Constant Complainer

Sometimes, Jesus, I feel guilty for all the things we have.

Don't feel guilty for those things, Lisa. Maybe just whisper a quiet "thank you" when you're recognizing how good you have it.

I guess the guilt comes in when I've overlooked these things and taken them for granted. Then I realize I've been a constant complainer.

Yeah, well...go ahead and feel guilty about that, Lisa.

Live Up To

We have a new employee at work, Jesus. His name is *Jesús*. I could never do that to my sons.

It's not like his mom named him Lee Harvey, Ann. Or Adolf. Or Judas.

Still, what a burden to put on a boy, Jesus. How do you live up to a name like that?

You call yourself a Christian, Ann.

How do *you* live up to *that*?

Really Inspired Me

Whatever happened to that one famous Christian singer, Jesus? The super hot chick with the long hair and the smokin' body...

Long tours away from her family, the pressure from her managers and record label, the "industry," Carl; it all became too much.

That's a shame.

She really inspired me to worship.

If you'll think about it, Carl, you *really* worshipped *her*.

And that kinda creeped her out.

© Radio Free Babylon

Do What I Do

Your ministry was marked by healing and liberation, Jesus.

Mine? I don't think they even hear a word I say.

You wouldn't believe the impact you're having lately, Joe. I field sincere, intense prayers from people you think are far gone.

Seriously? Like who?

Ha! I'm not letting this go to your head, Joe.

Just keep doing what you're doing and let me do what I do.

© Radio Free Babylon

Author and Finisher

My old friends from church, they say, "You'll be back." They're all, "God won't let you go, Kevin." I *hate* those trite phrases and platitudes–

Jesus?

Oh, you should've *seen* your face just then, Kevin!

But hey, know this: I'm the author, Kevin. And the finisher.

© Radio Free Babylon

When Pigs Fly
(Mark 5:13)

Your people, they don't love one another, Son of Man.

Far, *far* from it.

They'll get there, Satan.

Yeah, *right!*

When *pigs* fly!

Off a cliff and into the sea.

© Radio Free Babylon

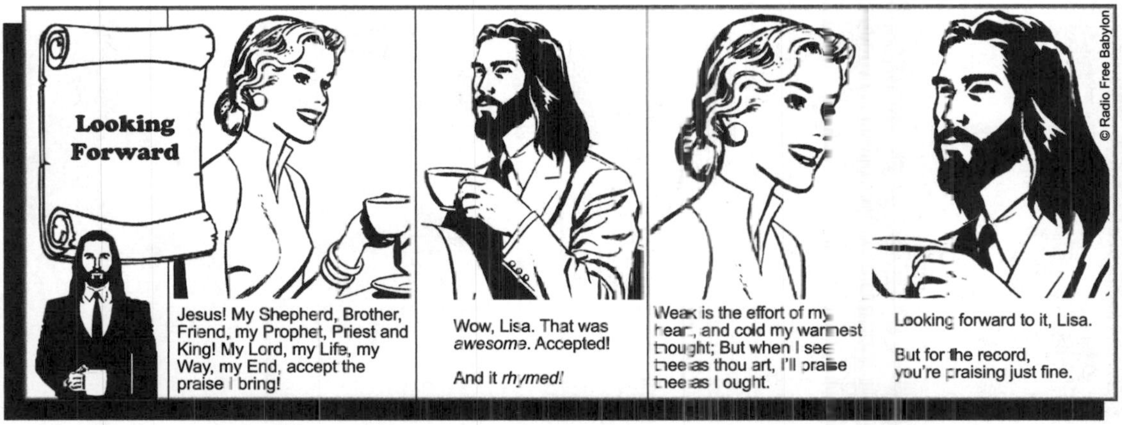
Looking Forward
Jesus! My Shepherd, Brother, Friend, my Prophet, Priest and King! My Lord, my Life, my Way, my End, accept the praise I bring!
Wow, Lisa. That was *awesome*. Accepted!
And it *rhymed!*
Weak is the effort of my heart, and cold my warmest thought; But when I see thee as thou art, I'll praise thee as I ought.
Looking forward to it, Lisa.
But for the record, you're praising just fine.
© Radio Free Babylon

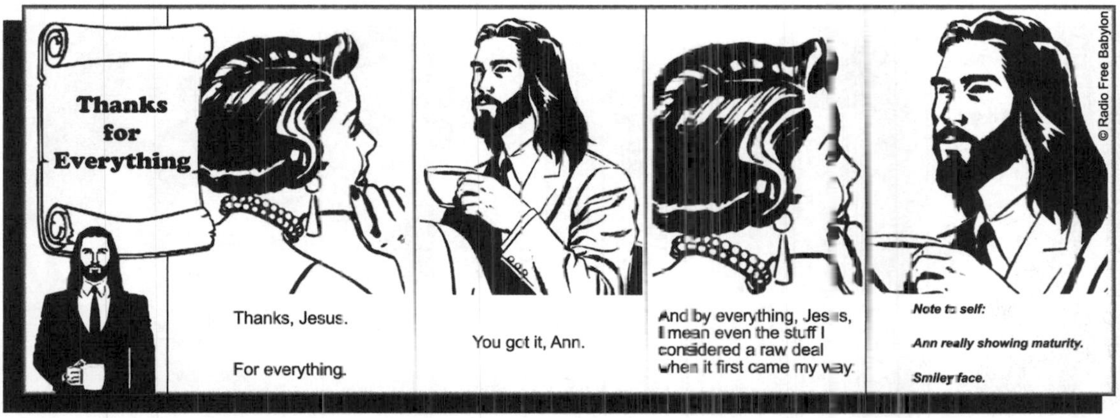
Thanks for Everything
Thanks, Jesus.
For everything.
You got it, Ann.
And by everything, Jesus, I mean even the stuff I considered a raw deal when it first came my way.
Note to self:
Ann really showing maturity.
Smiley face.
© Radio Free Babylon

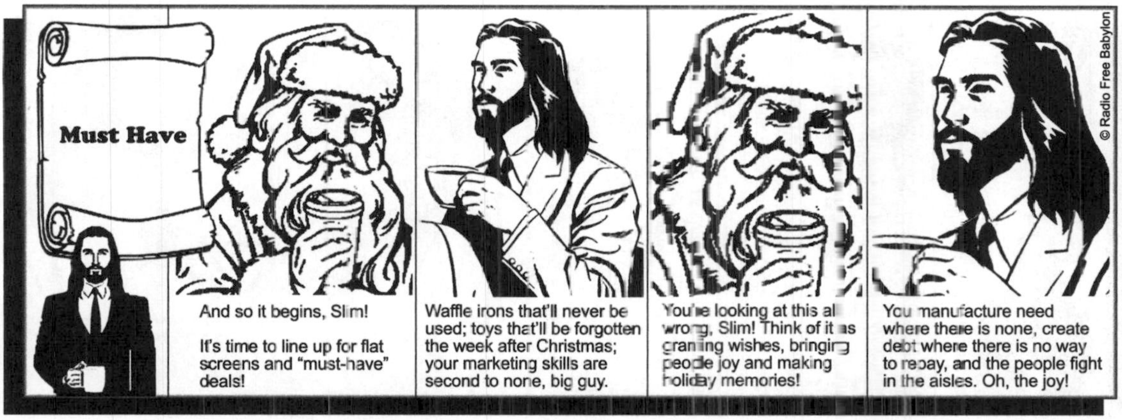
Must Have
And so it begins, Slim!
It's time to line up for flat screens and "must-have" deals!
Waffle irons that'll never be used; toys that'll be forgotten the week after Christmas; your marketing skills are second to none, big guy.
You're looking at this all wrong, Slim! Think of it as granting wishes, bringing people joy and making holiday memories!
You manufacture need where there is none, create debt where there is no way to repay, and the people fight in the aisles. Oh, the joy!
© Radio Free Babylon

Ouch, Jesus

I really like this: *Love is patient, love is kind. It does not envy, it does not boast, it is not proud. It does not dishonor others. It is not self-seeking.*

Good stuff there, Carl.

Now replace the word "love" with your own name and see how it sounds.

Carl is patient, Carl is kind. Carl...does not envy, Carl does not...boast, Carl...is not proud...*Ouch*, Jesus. This is...just...*not right*.

Yeah, it isn't, Carl.

Not yet, anyway.

A Very Real Loss

A family in my congregation had to put their dog down this week, Jesus. They're taking it pretty hard. How do I treat the death of a pet?

A dog is a member of the family, Joe. They give their love unconditionally. I'd suggest you mourn with them. It's a very real loss.

So you want me to treat the loss of a dog like a death in the family, Jesus?

C'mon, man! If I know when a sparrow falls, don't you think I'd know when a dog dies?

Ya know, you could use a pet.

Frowning Guy in the Sky

I just don't like the notion of some frowning Guy in the Sky waiting for me to screw up, Jesus, so he can banish me to everlasting flames!

There are three things wrong with that statement, Kevin:

#1 Eager to banish you. #2 Waiting for you to screw up.

You said three.

You've screwed up, Kevin, and you've banished yourself.

Yet God calls to you...smiling.

© Radio Free Babylon

No Need For You

Face it, Son of Man, you've been *replaced!* Thanks to man's innovations in science, he now regards *himself* as god! There's *no need* for you!

You can try to sell them on that, Satan, but when it comes down to it, they know better.

Nonsense! They can predict the weather! They can cure disease! They can travel in space! You are a *relic!* Unnecessary!

And yet every time there's so much as a power outage, who are they calling on?

Happy Holidays

And after she hands me my receipt, the clerk looks me right in the eye, smiles, and says, "Happy *Holidays!*" Can you *believe it*, Jesus?

Lisa, it's her company's policy. She didn't intend to offend you.

Or me.

Well, I let her know in no uncertain terms that she *did!* And I got right in her face and said, "Merry *CHRIST-mas!*"

Lisa–1. My cause–0.

My Needs

You know my needs, Jesus.

Yes, I do, Ann.

You know what I'm going to ask of you before I even ask.

Of course, Ann. And maybe someday your needs and what you ask of me will be the same thing.

East from West

So, I was reading in the Bible, Jesus, or rather, someone told me, or I heard it somewhere... whatever! *Anyway*...that you cast our sins far away. Right?

As far as the east is from the west, so far have I removed your transgressions from you, Carl.

Yeah, that's it!

So, that's like, what? New York to California?

Gonna be a little further than that, Carl.

You can't get there from here.

© Radio Free Babylon

Such a Hater

I don't need your *judgment*, Jesus! I don't want to walk around feeling guilty! Why do you have to be such a hater?

Whoa, Kevin! You got me all wrong! Everyone knows John 3:16, but they forget the next verse. I'm not here to condemn, but to save!

So, wait. Let me get my head around this...

You're...

I'm on *your side*, Kevin.

© Radio Free Babylon

Actually Ministering

I love me a handsome and debonair man in a sharp suit, preaching the gospel of wealth to an audience of people barely making it, Son of Man.

Because you see yourself in him, Satan. And for every one like him you can point to, I'll show you a thousand people actually ministering.

Oh, no need to trouble yourself, Boy King.

I know which side my bread is buttered on.

Yeah, well that butter has turned rancid.

And your bread is moldy.

© Radio Free Babylon

— 84 —

Thinking of You

It's supposed to be a season of peace, Jesus, yet every year it turns into this stressful, hectic time. I just want to let you know I'm thinking of you.

Sweet, Lisa. Thanks.

And I'd like to ask you to please help me get a good parking spot this morning at the mall. Got some last minute shopping to do.

For unto us a child is born, to us a son is given, and the government will be on his shoulders. And he will be called Parking Spot Finder.

God Bless 'Em

My kids, God bless 'em.

Pooled their money and bought me some silly thing I don't need and won't use.

And every time you look at that silly gift, Ann, you'll recall their hopeful, loving faces as you unwrapped it.

Well, of course, Jesus.

Wait...there's a lesson here somewhere, right?

God bless you.

Lead Us Not

...and lead us not into temptation, but deliver us from...*Hey, wait a minute!* Why would God ever "lead me into temptation," Jesus?

Unfortunate translation there from the Aramaic into the Greek, Carl. Think of it as "don't let us be tested." Sort of like how Job was tested.

Job got a raw deal, J-Man. That old dude was tested *big time.*

Lead me not *there*, OK?

The Book of Carl will read much milder, trust me.

But wherever I lead you... try to follow, Carl.

Weighing Me Down

My prayer life isn't peaceful at all, Jesus. To be totally honest with you, it stresses me out.

I hear you, Lisa. You come to me with your cares and concerns, holding them tight, anxious, fretting, worried.

I *bring them to you*, Jesus!

But I get no *relief*. They're *weighing me down!*

You're not hearing me, Lisa. You can bring them all day long.

I need you to leave them.

© Radio Free Babylon

The Primest

Youth is wasted on the young.

So they say, Carl, but kids don't think so.

In heaven, I hope I'm not this age. Please tell me we're all in our prime in heaven.

The primest, Carl. And that sour look of yours is nowhere to be found.

© Radio Free Babylon

Staring Contest

Staring contest!

Ready? Go!

Not playing, Satan.

I win! I win!

Haha!

Imaginary victories were always your thing.

© Radio Free Babylon

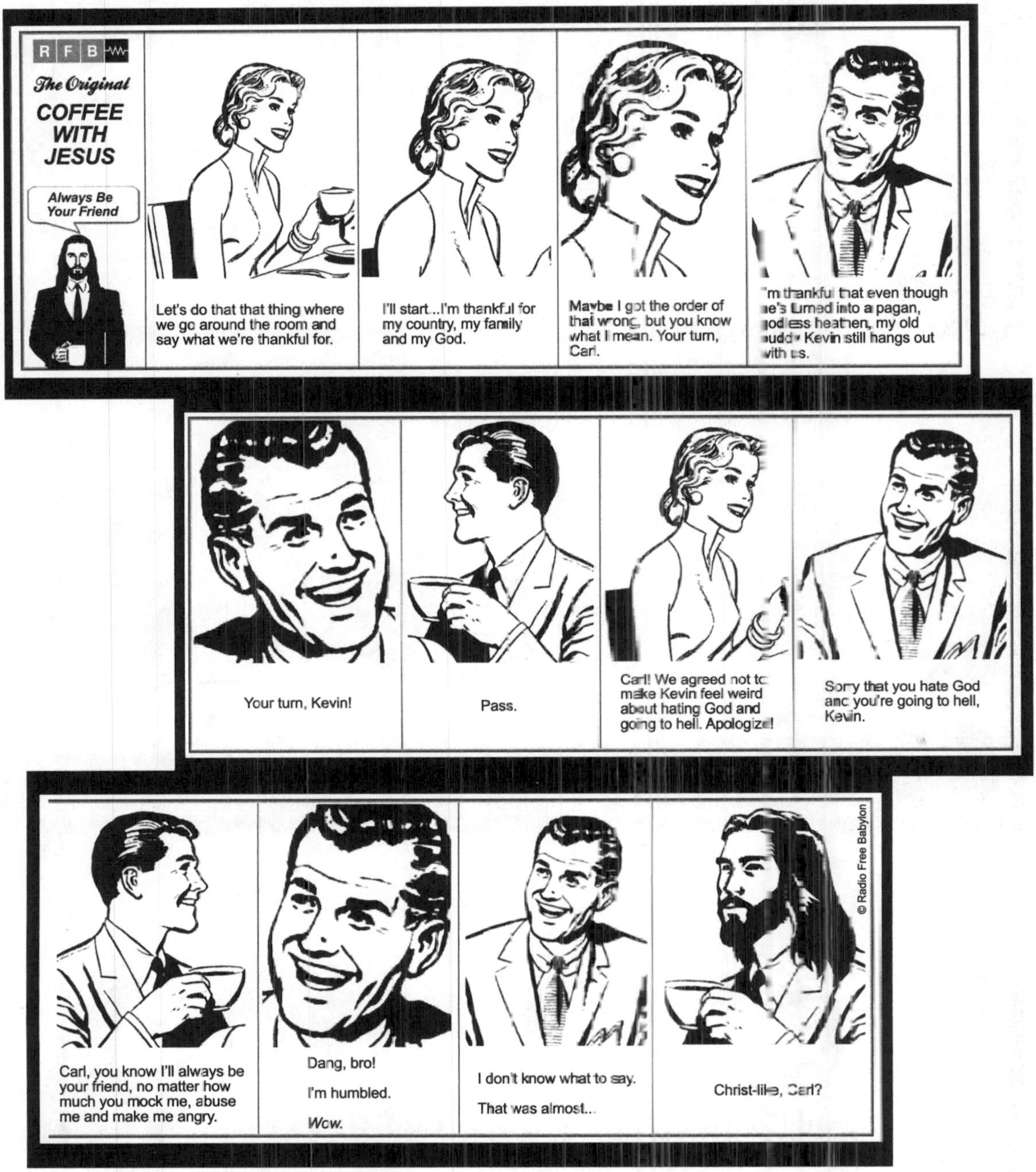
RFB
The Original
COFFEE WITH JESUS
Always Be Your Friend
Let's do that that thing where we go around the room and say what we're thankful for.
I'll start...I'm thankful for my country, my family and my God.
Maybe I got the order of that wrong, but you know what I mean. Your turn, Carl.
I'm thankful that even though he's turned into a pagan, godless heathen, my old buddy Kevin still hangs out with us.
Your turn, Kevin!
Pass.
Carl! We agreed not to make Kevin feel weird about hating God and going to hell. Apologize!
Sorry that you hate God and you're going to hell, Kevin.
Carl, you know I'll always be your friend, no matter how much you mock me, abuse me and make me angry.
Dang, bro!
I'm humbled.
Wow.
I don't know what to say.
That was almost...
Christ-like, Carl?
© Radio Free Babylon

Grant Your Wishes

With God, all things are possible. You said so yourself, Jesus.

Indeed I did, Lisa.

But God is not obliged to grant your wishes.

Nope! Not gonna give in to the negative! I'm holding on to that promise!

All things are possible!

Possible doesn't equate to probable, Lisa.

I promise.

Too Literally

You give them false hope, Son of Man! *Never once* have I seen one of your people cast a mountain into the sea! What sort of nonsense was *that*?

You take things too literally, Satan.

Excuse me for thinking the Boy King meant what he said! So, maybe the whole bottomless pit, lake of fire thing is just symbolism?

Wouldn't that be nice for you?

Nope, that one's literal.

I Want to Find

Why is it so much easier for me to imagine that you are angry with me rather than pleased, Jesus?

Good question, Ann.

Perhaps you're not pleased with yourself.

*Ohhhh...*I want to find that place. I want to find that peace. I want to find...

I don't know, Jesus!

Don't make it difficult, Ann.

Just find my smile.

Know Show Go

It'd sure be helpful, Jesus, if I could get some kind of job performance review from you. It's difficult from where I stand, to know if I'm being effective.

It's one thing to know the path, Joe, and another thing to show the path. And an altogether harder thing to go the path.

Ummm...

What?

You're three for three, Joe.

I'm going to keep you on.

Look Forward to Sundays

Just being totally honest here, Jesus, and I know it's not right, but I look forward to Sundays more for football than anything else.

I appreciate your honesty, Carl. Football has become something of a religion in this country.

So, my buddy Jake has tickets to the game and he asked me to go and I just wanna make sure you're cool with me missing...

And church has become something of a sport in this country.

The Choice Wine

Some say that the wine you made at the wedding was non-alcoholic, Jesus.

Explain *"Everyone brings out the choice wine first and then the cheaper wine after the guests have had too much to drink,"* Lisa.

Your wine was choice.

And everyone was drunk.

don't dabble, Lisa.

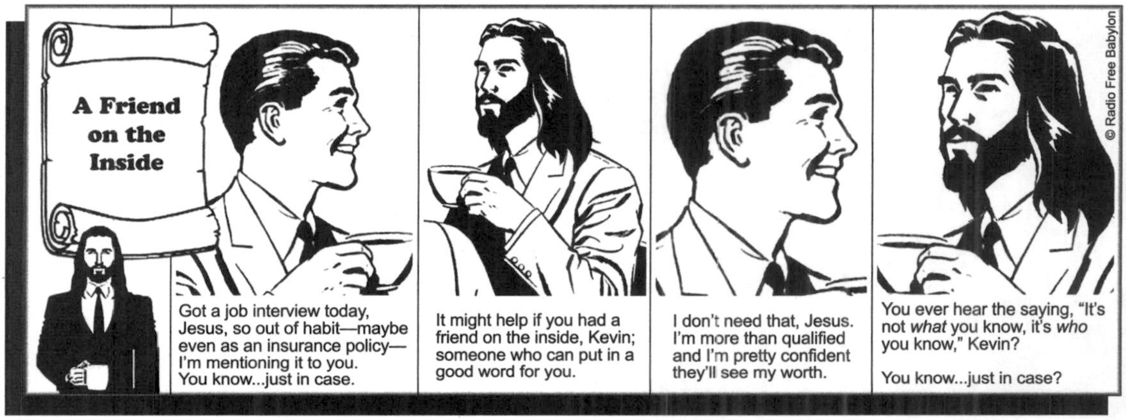
A Friend on the Inside
Got a job interview today, Jesus, so out of habit—maybe even as an insurance policy—I'm mentioning it to you. You know...just in case.
It might help if you had a friend on the inside, Kevin; someone who can put in a good word for you.
I don't need that, Jesus. I'm more than qualified and I'm pretty confident they'll see my worth.
You ever hear the saying, "It's not *what* you know, it's *who* you know," Kevin?
You know...just in case?
© Radio Free Babylon

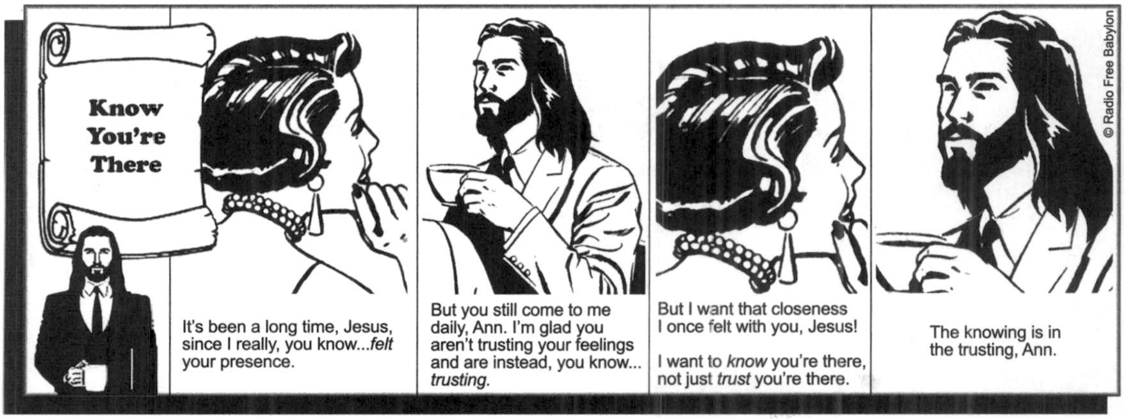
Know You're There
It's been a long time, Jesus, since I really, you know...*felt* your presence.
But you still come to me daily, Ann. I'm glad you aren't trusting your feelings and are instead, you know... *trusting*.
But I want that closeness I once felt with you, Jesus!
I want to *know* you're there, not just *trust* you're there.
The knowing is in the trusting, Ann.
© Radio Free Babylon

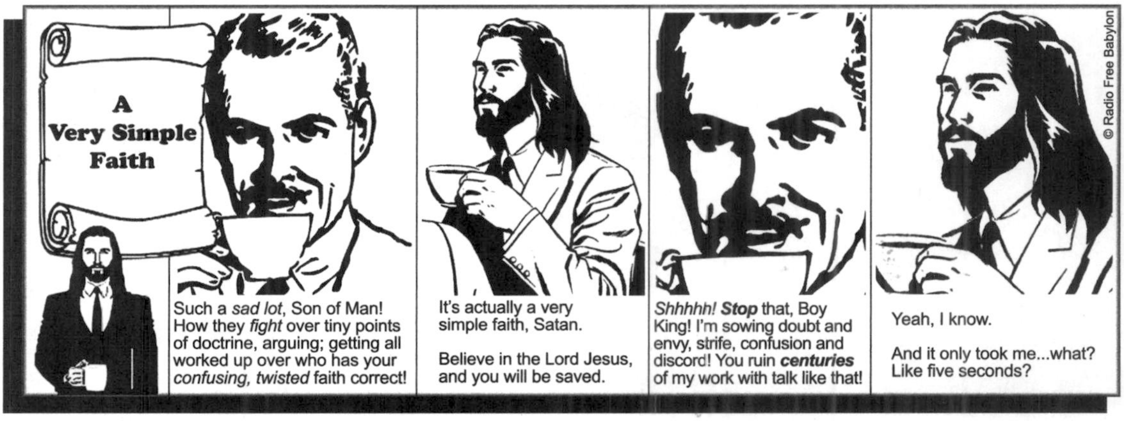
A Very Simple Faith
Such a *sad lot*, Son of Man! How they *fight* over tiny points of doctrine, arguing; getting all worked up over who has your *confusing, twisted* faith correct!
It's actually a very simple faith, Satan.
Believe in the Lord Jesus, and you will be saved.
Shhhhh! ***Stop*** that, Boy King! I'm sowing doubt and envy, strife, confusion and discord! You ruin ***centuries*** of my work with talk like that!
Yeah, I know.
And it only took me...what? Like five seconds?
© Radio Free Babylon

This is My Father's World

Help me reconcile this, Jesus. The Bible says the world is six thousand years old, and yet scientists say it's almost five billion years old.

Technically, the Bible doesn't say that, Carl.

But either way, this is my Father's world.

You're not helping.

You sure about that?

Eternally Grateful

...and if that thing I've been asking you for...if it should come to pass, Jesus, you know I'd be eternally grateful.

Experience tells us you'll be grateful for about two weeks, Lisa. Then your focus will turn to the next thing you're asking me for.

Wait, like my kids two weeks after Christmas, Jesus? The toys they so wanted now abandoned in the back of the closet?

Kinda like, Lisa, yep.

Ya know, we could be moving mountains, but you're asking me for trinkets.

Some Wise Advice

I try to remember, "If you don't have anything nice to say, don't say anything at all."

That's some wise advice.

That's a quote from the character Thumper in the Disney movie *Bambi*, Joe, and it doesn't apply in a lot of cases.

So, you don't think it's wise advice, Jesus?

Oh, it's great advice, Joe.

If you're a baby rabbit in a cartoon forest.

Give This Stuff Away

And for only twenty dollars per DVD, Jesus, I'll gain spiritual insights and special knowledge through the courses they offer.

Spiritual insights that come with a pricetag on them are pretty well worthless, Ann. And it's only $19.95, by the way. You saved a nickel!

They need to fund their ministry, Jesus!

They can't just *give* this stuff away!

All you need to know is right here, Ann.

And I've never charged you a dime.

He'll Come Around

I respect that my ex-wife wants to raise our son to believe in you, Jesus, but he's also going to hear my side. I want him to be open-minded.

So you don't "respect" your ex-wife's faith or her wishes at all, Kevin. You're only going to confuse the boy. I'd suggest you keep quiet.

He'll be confused for a little bit, sure, just like I was, but eventually he'll come around to my way of thinking.

A millstone makes a really poor flotation device, Kevin.

Silly, Passing, Political Argument

One of my oldest friends has been posting stupid, politically ignorant things on Facebook, Jesus. We've been arguing in the comments a lot lately.

It'd be a shame to lose an old friend over some silly, passing, political argument, Carl.

Tell me about it, Jesus! He's being such an *idiot!* It's *eating me up* inside!

What should I *do?*

Uhhh...quit arguing?

You Totally Get It

Some days, Jesus, I just long for it to be over. I'm so *spent*, worn, tired and had *enough!* I can't wait to get home and take a nap! I'm sorry.

Sometimes you have to dismiss the crowd and row to the other side of the lake just to get alone, Joe. Don't be sorry. Ministry's tough.

You totally *get it*, Jesus.

I *love* that about you.

Beer here, brother.

And it'd be a pretty low-rent god that *didn't* get it, Joe.

One of Us

No offense, Jesus, but wasn't it just a little *easy* for you to walk the earth in human form?

Not just form, Lisa, but substance as well. I was a man of sorrows, acquainted with grief, tempted in every way, just as you are.

So, it's like...you're *one of us!*

I didn't call myself "Son of man" over eighty times for nothing, Lisa.

This Isn't News

So many out there claiming to know you, Son of Man, but by their actions they deny you.

Not everyone who says to me, "Lord, Lord," will enter the Kingdom of Heaven, Satan. This isn't news.

They call to you, Boy King, and you turn them away?

And they say *I'm* the cruel one.

People trying to get through security with forged passports know the risks, Satan. It won't be news to them either.

© Radio Free Babylon

Receiving the Blessings

I try to live right, to please you, Jesus, and yet I don't seem to be receiving the blessings that are promised in the Bible. I'm getting depressed.

I don't want you depressed, Ann, but I shouldn't need to point out to you how very blessed you already are.

So, you're saying I'm just being a big *baby*, Jesus? Is *that* it?

Maybe, kinda...OK, yes.

You wanna be blessed, Ann? Be a blessing.

Living in the Past

The field is so much bigger on the dating sites now that I'm not limiting myself to these *Kumbaya*-singing good girls.

Were you dating women trapped in a temporal loop in the space-time continuum, Kevin? No one has sung *Kumbaya* in years.

Funny, Jesus, but now that you mention it, anyone who subscribes to your dogmatic, exclusionary religion *is* living in the past.

Said the man who's been stalking his old high school girlfriends on Facebook.

Step-by-Step Directions

You know where I've been, Jesus, where I'm heading. Can't you just slip me a little hint about how to, you know, stay on the right path?

If I provided you with step-by-step directions for your life, Carl, would you follow them?

Absolutely! That'd be awesome! No more wondering. No more questioning! I'd love that!

Alright then, Carl. Here ya go:

Follow me.

Playing with Fire

I think one of my counselees might be forming a crush on me, Jesus.

Oh, you *think*. .she *might?*

Let's not play games here, Joe. The truth, please.

Alright, OK, Jesus. It's a fully formed crush...and the truth is...well...I find myself looking forward to her appointments.

Very good, Joe. Thanks.

I think Sparky the Fire Dog put it well when he said, "Stop, drop and roll."

A Living Body

The Bible says that your people are like different parts of a body. Some are hands, some are feet, some ears, and some eyes, right, Jesus?

Yep. Each part contributing to the whole, Lisa. A living body, everyone with a part to play.

Well, I think I know a few people who'd be good candidates to be the...

The roles aren't permanent, Lisa.

Everyone's one of those once in a while.

I Get Bored Reading The Bible

How do I put this, Jesus? I get *bored* reading the Bible. It's so long. It's so vast, so sprawling. Not to mention daunting and confusing.

You read all the *Game of Thrones* books, Ann; just as vast, almost three times as long, yet you were riveted the entire time.

That's different, Jesus. It had lust for power, complex genealogies, swordplay, dragons kings, queens, triumph and tragedy.

Check, check, check, check, check, check, check and check, Ann.

Oh...plus redemption.

They're a Joke

Your people are *so weak,* Son of Man, and *foolish!* They're a *joke!*

I *laugh* at them! And *YOU!*

Well, God has chosen the foolish things of the world to confound the wise, Satan. And...where they are weak, I am strong.

You speak in *circles,* Boy King! What does that even *mean?*

Talk to me plainly!

It means the joke's on you.

How Much Dignity

I got my *dignity,* Jesus! I'm not gonna stand by and let these know-nothings walk all over me, tellin' me what to do!

How much dignity, Carl, do you think a man nailed naked to a cross has?

Whoa, Jesus.

Don't put that on me.

I'm not, Carl.

It's on me.

So suck it up, OK?

On the Guest List

If I could have three dinner guests from all the people in history, Jesus, I'd definitely include you on the guest list.

Thanks, Kevin. I'll even do the dishes. Then we can watch SportsCenter. I'll just crash on the couch. And wait'll you try my grilled fish for breakfast!

Uh...how long you planning on staying?

As long as you'll have me, Kevin. *Hey!* Maybe over the weekend we can clean out the closet in your spare bedroom. What a mess!

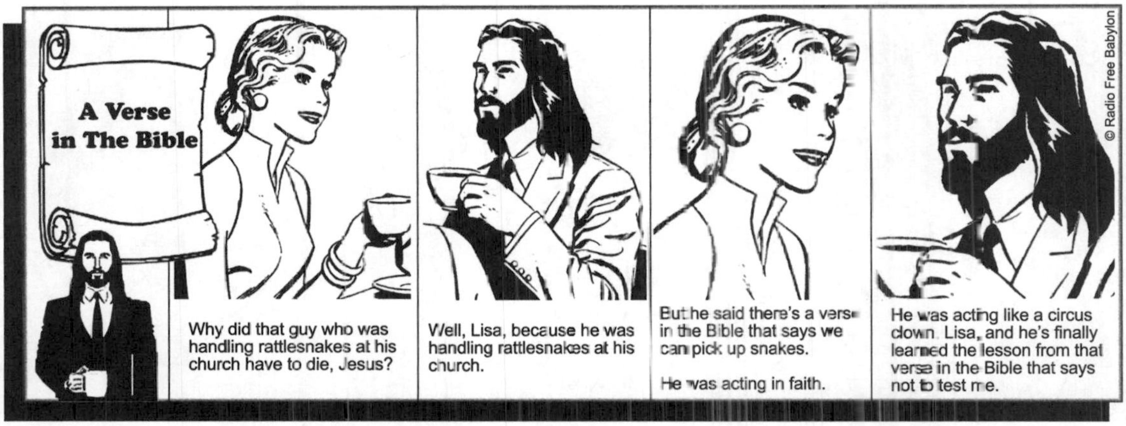
A Verse in The Bible
Why did that guy who was handling rattlesnakes at his church have to die, Jesus?
Well, Lisa, because he was handling rattlesnakes at his church.
But he said there's a verse in the Bible that says we can pick up snakes.
He was acting in faith.
He was acting like a circus clown, Lisa, and he's finally learned the lesson from that verse in the Bible that says not to test me.
© Radio Free Babylon

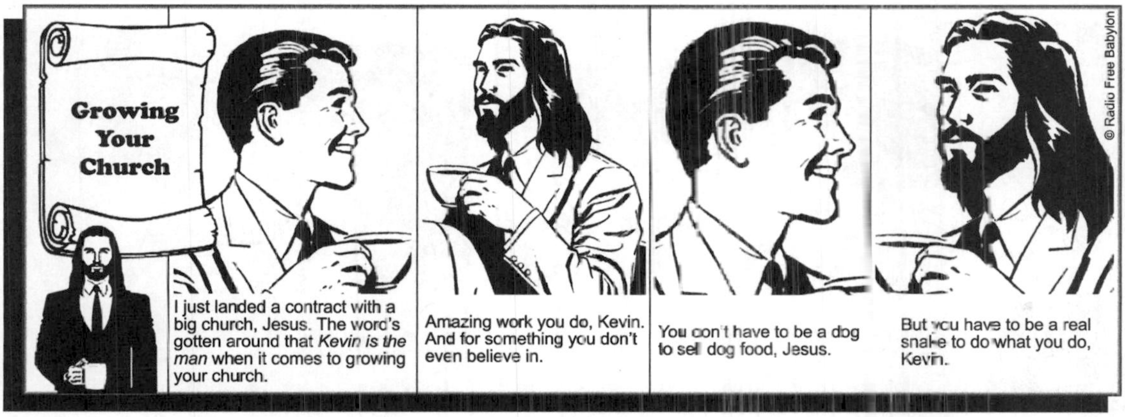
Growing Your Church
I just landed a contract with a big church, Jesus. The word's gotten around that *Kevin is the man* when it comes to growing your church.
Amazing work you do, Kevin. And for something you don't even believe in.
You don't have to be a dog to sell dog food, Jesus.
But you have to be a real snake to do what you do, Kevin.
© Radio Free Babylon

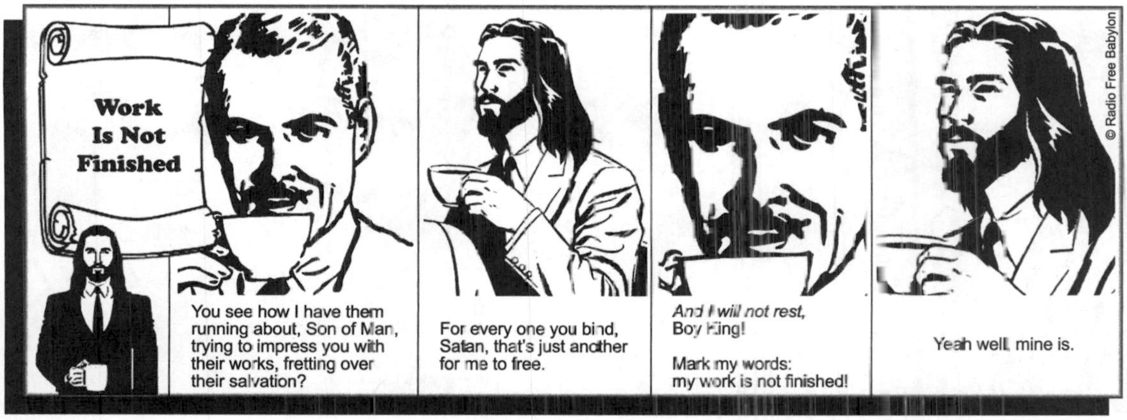
Work Is Not Finished
You see how I have them running about, Son of Man, trying to impress you with their works, fretting over their salvation?
For every one you bind, Satan, that's just another for me to free.
And I will not rest, Boy King!
Mark my words: my work is not finished!
Yeah well, mine is.
© Radio Free Babylon

Going Pretty Good

Sometimes, Jesus, when things are going pretty good, I get this weird feeling that something bad must be about to happen.

So, like when your crops are coming along nicely, you feel like maybe your son might be pressed into service by tribal warlords after they kill you?

So, things are going pretty good, Lisa?

It's My Time

I want to have *my best life now*, Jesus.

Not every day can be a Friday, Ann.

But *it's my time!* I want to become a *better me!*

This isn't about you, Ann.

You're doing it wrong.

Flat-Out Boring

How is it that my days seem to drag on forever and yet the years seem to fly by so quickly, Jesus?

When you aren't taking time to appreciate the little things, you can easily miss the big things, Carl.

This is that whole "live in the moment" wishy-washy nonsense, Jesus. Nobody actually does that. Life is sometimes flat-out boring.

Especially when it's unappreciated, Carl.

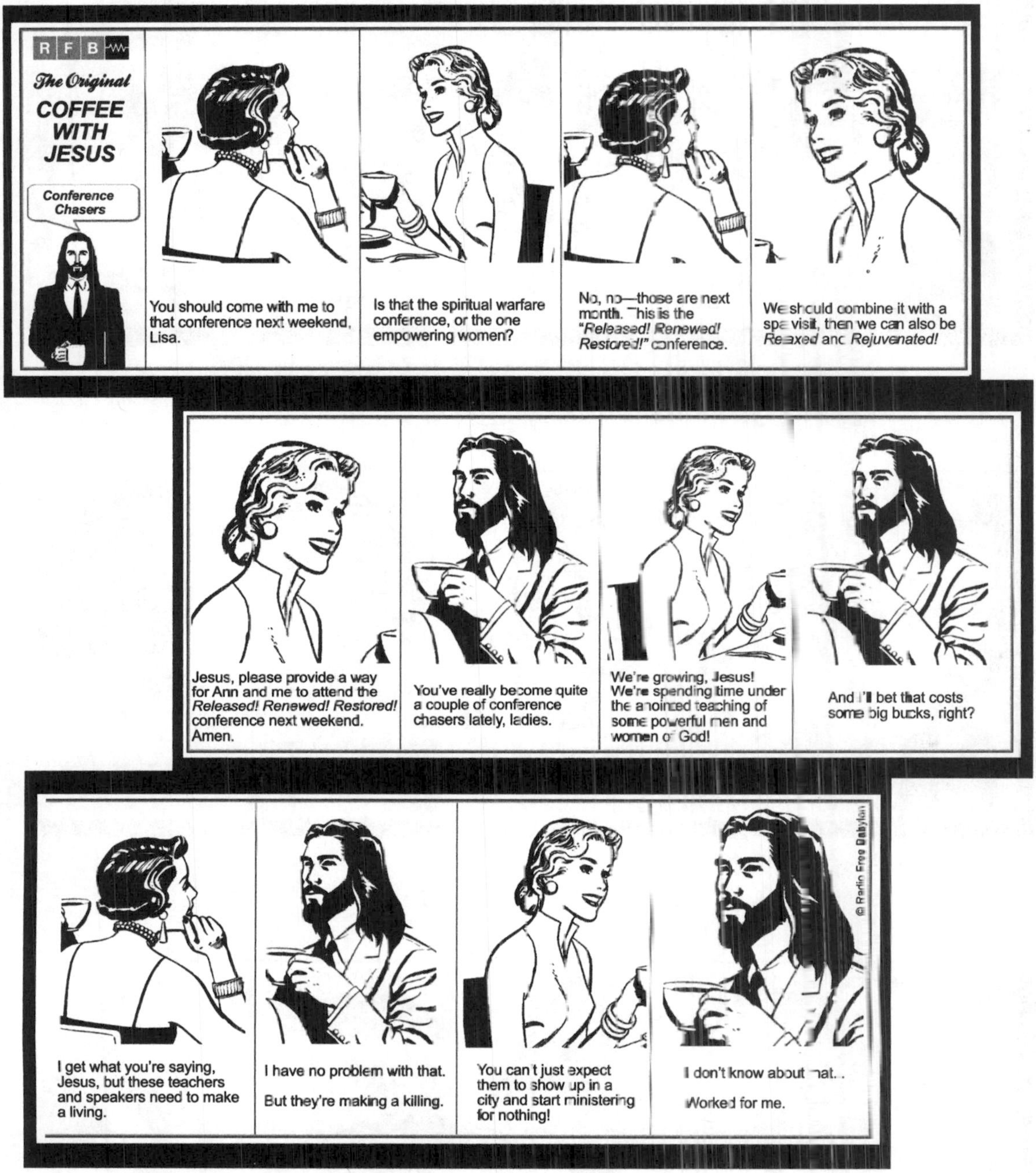
RFB
The Original
COFFEE WITH JESUS
Conference Chasers
You should come with me to that conference next weekend, Lisa.
Is that the spiritual warfare conference, or the one empowering women?
No, no—those are next month. This is the "Released! Renewed! Restored!" conference.
We should combine it with a spa visit, then we can also be Relaxed and Rejuvenated!
Jesus, please provide a way for Ann and me to attend the Released! Renewed! Restored! conference next weekend. Amen.
You've really become quite a couple of conference chasers lately, ladies.
We're growing, Jesus! We're spending time under the anointed teaching of some powerful men and women of God!
And I'll bet that costs some big bucks, right?
I get what you're saying, Jesus, but these teachers and speakers need to make a living.
I have no problem with that.
But they're making a killing.
You can't just expect them to show up in a city and start ministering for nothing!
I don't know about that...
Worked for me.
© Radio Free Babylon

Ungrateful, Horrible Babies

You see it, Son of Man. Don't deny it. They're rotten. They're spoiled. They're ungrateful, horrible babies!

You and I see things differently, Satan.

Oh, please, Boy King!

They're whining brats!

One father's brat is another Father's child.

The World is Broken

The world is broken, Jesus.

How can we fix it, Lisa?

Well, I think people need to look inside themselves and try to find their best self and seek to bring that side out.

No, Lisa, that's *why* the world is broken, not how we fix it.

Quite a Ways

I feel like you're urging me in a certain direction, Jesus.

And I'm pleased that you're moving in that direction, Ann.

Alright then, you've got me where you want me.

Now what?

Where I want you is quite a ways down the road, Ann.

So keep moving.

They're Being Saved

I haven't seen anyone saved in my church in half a year, Jesus. This is really getting discouraging.

Do you need to see crying people kneeling down front Joe, confessing their sins, wooed by soft music and pleading words?

I've always wanted to say, "I see that hand! I see that hand! The buses will wait. The buses will wait. I see that hand." Maybe not, huh?

Yeah, maybe not.

And they're being saved, Joe, whether you see it or not.

A Mighty Thing

I'm so sick of all the haters critcizing Pastor Steve.

God is doing a mighty thing at Worship World.

Am I, Ann? Or is Pastor Steve wooing people from other churches, building a monument to his own ego through clever marketing?

Well, pardon me, Jesus, but now you just sound like one of the haters.

Weird...

I said that in love, Ann.

Love the Sinner

My stance on it is this, Jesus: love the sinner, hate the sin.

I'll do you one better, Carl: love the sinner, hate your own sin.

So, I guess you have some work to do?

Subpar Sunday School Schlock

Ecchh! Another film is out where you're a handsome white guy with a British accent! It's all such subpar Sunday School schlock!

You hate any retelling of my story, Satan, so your critique is suspect.

But do go on.

It's *horrible!* Unknown cast, laughable CGI, made-for-TV production values! I've seen better *puppet shows!* I give it...*ZERO stars!*

Despised by the in-the-know critics, and yet the great unwashed crowd flocks to see it.

History repeats itself.

His Craftsmanship

It's so cool that all these new planets are being discovered every day by NASA!

Very cool, Kevin. The heavens proclaim the glory of God. The skies display his craftsmanship.

Please, don't start on that whole creation myth with me, Jesus. This is mankind uncovering the mysteries of the universe!

Fine, Kevin, but as you Google, *"How many stars are there?"* and get no helpful answers, get this: I know every one of them by name.

More Than We Can Handle

God will never give us more than we can handle, isn't that right, Jesus?

The verse you're thinking of is often misquoted, Lisa. God will not let you be *tempted* beyond what you can bear.

Oh, that's a bit different.

So, God might give us more than we can handle?

It can often feel that way, Lisa, absolutely.

Until you let me handle it.

In Jesus' Name

...and I ask all these things in Jesus' name.

Amen!

Ann, tacking "in Jesus' name" to the end of your prayers doesn't obligate me to give you what you ask for. They aren't magic words.

It says in the Bible, "You may ask me for anything in my name, and I will do it," Jesus.

Think of it as, "for Jesus' sake" instead, Ann, and maybe you'll start to see how your selfish desires don't really line up with my name.

Not So Innocent

We all know you love "the little children of the world," Jesus, but what about...you know...everyone else? Like...the not-so-innocent?

Especially them, Carl.

It's the sick who need a doctor.

I'm not talking about physical healing, Jesus.

Can you make them... *innocent* again?

Red and yellow, black and white.

Spotless, Carl.

Honest Agnostic

Funny how all my former Christian "friends" have stopped wanting to hang out with me, isn't it, Jesus?

Well, Kevin, when you were an honest agnostic, that was one thing, but you're turning into an annoying antagonist. It gets old.

Some one you got there, Jesus! Get rid of the guy with questions! Throw out the honest seeker! Away with the man trying to *think!*

Question, Kevin, by all means! And yeah, *seek!* And please, *think!*

Just do it honestly again.

A Christian Audience

They made **seven** different versions of that *Noah* movie, Jesus, trying to find one they could sell to a Christian audience.

Paramount wants those *Passion of the Christ* dollars, Joe. Pandering to a Christian audience is *huuuuuge* business.

Then they should've done it in Hebrew with subtitles.

And maybe stayed a little more faithful to the story.

Doesn't bother me, Joe. Everyone's talking about it.

And even if Paramount doesn't profit from it, I will.

Fred Phelps

Fred Phelps gave Christians a bad name, Jesus. I'm not sorry he's dead. I'm kind of glad, to be honest.

Lisa...

Oh, wow...

I sounded a lot like Fred Phelps just then, Jesus.

Scary, isn't it, Lisa?

Life is Good

Life is good, Jesus.

So you say today, Ann.

What about later; maybe a few months from now?

Oh no! What's happening in a few months, Jesus?

Do I lose my job? Will I get sick? *Ohhhhhhhh...*

These are possibilities, Ann.

So remember...life is good.

Not for Nothing

It feels good to know that you're smiling down on me all day long, Jesus.

When your child is playing in traffic, Carl, or shouting in your face, or running from you when you're calling him to you, are you smiling?

OK, OK, J-Man. Point made. *Dang!*

You don't have to be so *harsh,* bro!

Not for nothing, Carl, but back in the day, they used to call me, "Teacher."

Jesus Freaks

Remember when they used to call people "Jesus Freaks," Jesus?

I sure do, Joe. First century. Reformation. Great revivals. 1970s.

Good times, those.

So why can't we be known again for our love, zeal and compassion, Jesus?

Not so much our politics.

You're preachin' to the choir, brother.

We should get on this.

A Form of Godliness

For every new congregation springing up in a city, I can show you ten dead or dying churches within twenty miles of it, Son of Man.

There's a time to plant and a time for uprooting, Satan.

Open your eyes, Boy King!

They possess a form of godliness, but deny the power thereof!

Hence the uprooting, silly.

© Radio Free Babylon

Takes Some Faith

That argument that you were either a liar, a lunatic or Lord is stupid, Jesus. First, we're forced to assume that the gospel records are accurate.

Yeah, that takes some faith.

Then, we have to accept that you're not just a *legend. Or...* maybe you *were* a lunatic who said true things sometimes!

My favorite part of this little exercise, Kevin, is that a guy so determined to deny my existence still wants to talk with me.

You Can Do This

You know that thing I gave up for Lent, Jesus? I think I'd be better off if I didn't take it up again come Easter.

I concur, Lisa. Forty days is plenty of time to get used to being without something. You can do this. In fact, you *already did it!*

Funny. I thought I'd miss that expensive spa, but this cheaper one in my neighborhood is almost as good.

We've a long way to go, Lisa.

But hey, this is progress.

Morally Failing

I know I *should* pray for him, Jesus, but I find it *very hard* to pray for that man.

Go ahead and say your ex-husband's name, Ann. You might find that helpful as you pray for his best. *And* as you work to forgive him.

Jim! I find it very hard to pray for—let alone forgive, Jesus—the adulterous, philandering—*oh, sorry*— "morally failing" *Jim!*

It's the catch-all phrase used to disguise the grievousness of the offense, Ann.

One more thing to forgive.

Commonality

And I was like, "Dude! Where do *you* get off tellin' me what is and what isn't "Christian"? I got a direct line to Jesus! He's my *boy!*"

First of all, Carl, I'm not your boy. You're mine. Secondly, I want you to find commonality with your brothers. It's utterly fruitless to struggle as you do.

"Commonality" is a code word for *compromise,* Jesus! I won't give up the faith! I will stand firm!

And I love that about you, Carl. What I don't love is your firm belief and assurance that I think exactly like you do.

Hollow Easter Bunny

Even though I don't subscribe to your faith anymore, Jesus, I still kinda look forward to my mom sending me a basketful of chocolates with a card.

Traditions are great, Kevin. They connect us to our past, to what matters. I'm glad your mom still does that for you.

But in recent years she's been sending the hollow Easter bunny instead of the solid one. That's kinda sad.

A subtle message on your mom's part, Kevin. God bless her.

It Is Finished

You *tricked* me, Son of Man! I kept thinking, "Why is he *allowing* this?" And by the time I realized what your plan was, it was too late.

I alluded to my resurrection numerous times throughout my ministry, Satan. You just didn't listen. Not that it would've mattered if you had.

You and your father played me well, Boy King, I'll give you that. But this isn't over! I'm not finished yet!

Yeah, maybe not. But *it* is.

More Like You

I'm going to do my best this morning not to judge all the extra people who decided to show up to church just for Easter, Jesus.

Thanks, Lisa.

Personally, I love when the extra people show up.

I wish I had your Spirit, Jesus.

Make me more like you!

That's a bold, dangerous, and beautiful prayer, Lisa.

Happy Easter to me.

© Radio Free Babylon

Seek My Counsel

And another thing, Jesus: Why even pray? If God is God and in control, then what's the point?

Let's imagine, Kevin, that you're in regular contact with me. At a certain point, you're faced with a decision and you seek my counsel.

I'm capable of weighing my options and deciding what's right and what's wrong. Not sure I need the help of an imaginary friend.

Before your first wedding, Kevin, do you remember those intense feelings of doubt? Say hello to your imaginary friend.

© Radio Free Babylon

Give Us This Day

It feels a little disingenuous for me to pray, "Give us this day our daily bread," Jesus, when I've got a refrigerator and a freezer full of food.

That means your food is only a power outage away from not being there, Carl.

That's why I bought the 20,000 watt whole house generator, Jesus. We'll even have TV and A/C!

Fine then, Carl. Come a power outage, I'll expect you to be the guy opening your home to everyone else without TV, A/C and food, OK?

© Radio Free Babylon

The Printed Word

Before the printing press, people didn't have Bibles in their homes, Jesus, so that's like 1500 years of people not having the printed Word.

And it's only been in the last two hundred years or so, Lisa, that literacy has been widespread. And that's just in the first world.

Then you know what I'm getting at, Jesus.

How were people saved?

In the beginning was the Word, Lisa.

Much, much later came the printing press.

A Glimpse

Can you give me a glimpse, Jesus, of what it will be like in Paradise?

I gave you many glimpses in the Scriptures, Joe, but OK... You know how you scream for joy on a roller coaster, laughing and shouting?

So, it'll be like that?

You said a glimpse, Joe.

You can't handle what it will *really* be like.

Coherent and Courteous

I have certain inalienable rights, Jesus, and when those rights are being trampled, I'm going to stand up and speak my mind forcefully!

No, you're not, Carl. You're going to sit down and deliver your thoughts in a coherent and courteous manner.

That's not how this works, Jesus. I can't sit idly by and just watch my country go to hell.

No, Carl, you'd rather actively participate in sending it there.

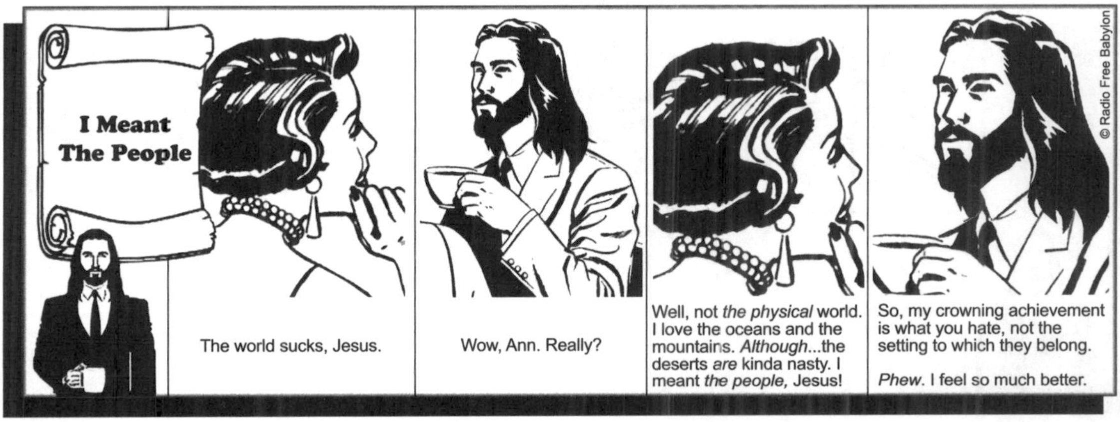
I Meant The People
The world sucks, Jesus.
Wow, Ann. Really?
Well, not *the physical* world. I love the oceans and the mountains. *Although*...the deserts *are* kinda nasty. I meant *the people,* Jesus!
So, my crowning achievement is what you hate, not the setting to which they belong.
Phew. I feel so much better.
© Radio Free Babylon

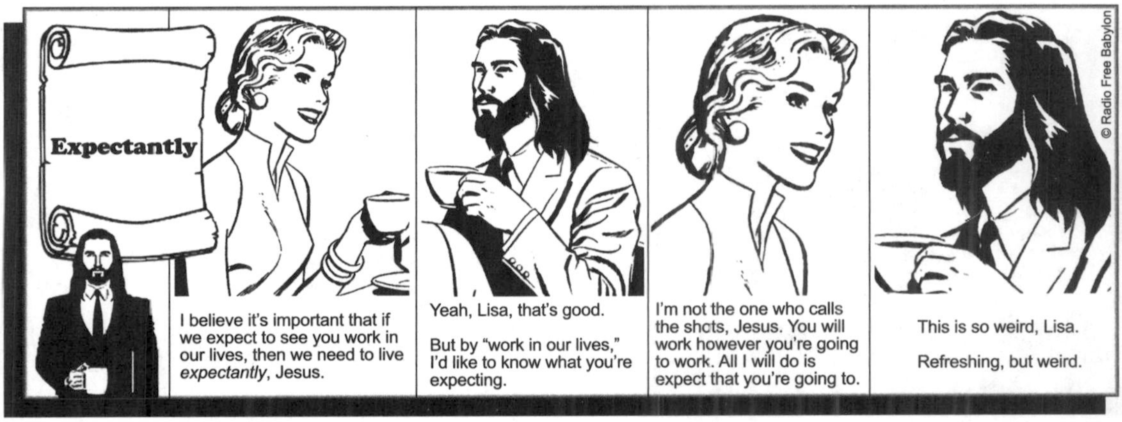
Expectantly
I believe it's important that if we expect to see you work in our lives, then we need to live *expectantly*, Jesus.
Yeah, Lisa, that's good.
But by "work in our lives," I'd like to know what you're expecting.
I'm not the one who calls the shots, Jesus. You will work however you're going to work. All I will do is expect that you're going to.
This is so weird, Lisa.
Refreshing, but weird.
© Radio Free Babylon

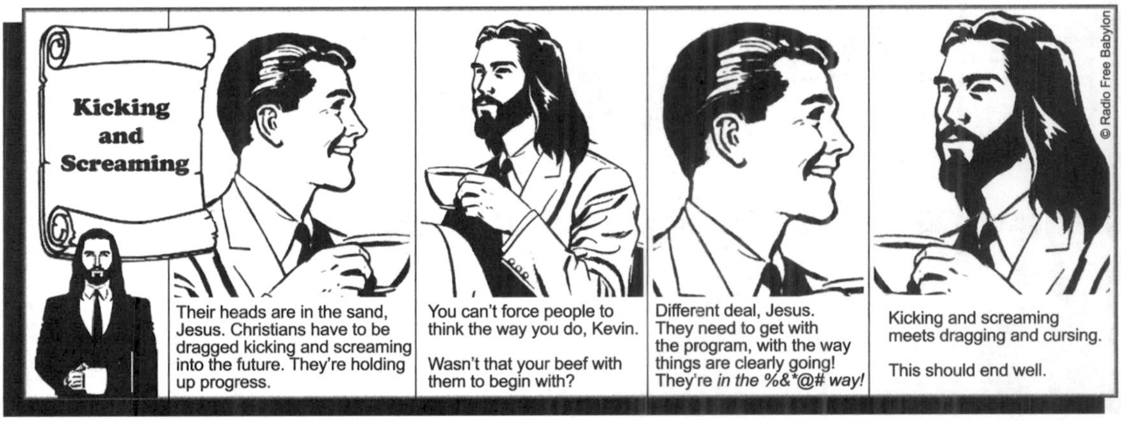
Kicking and Screaming
Their heads are in the sand, Jesus. Christians have to be dragged kicking and screaming into the future. They're holding up progress.
You can't force people to think the way you do, Kevin.
Wasn't that your beef with them to begin with?
Different deal, Jesus. They need to get with the program, with the way things are clearly going! They're *in the %&*@# way!*
Kicking and screaming meets dragging and cursing.
This should end well.
© Radio Free Babylon

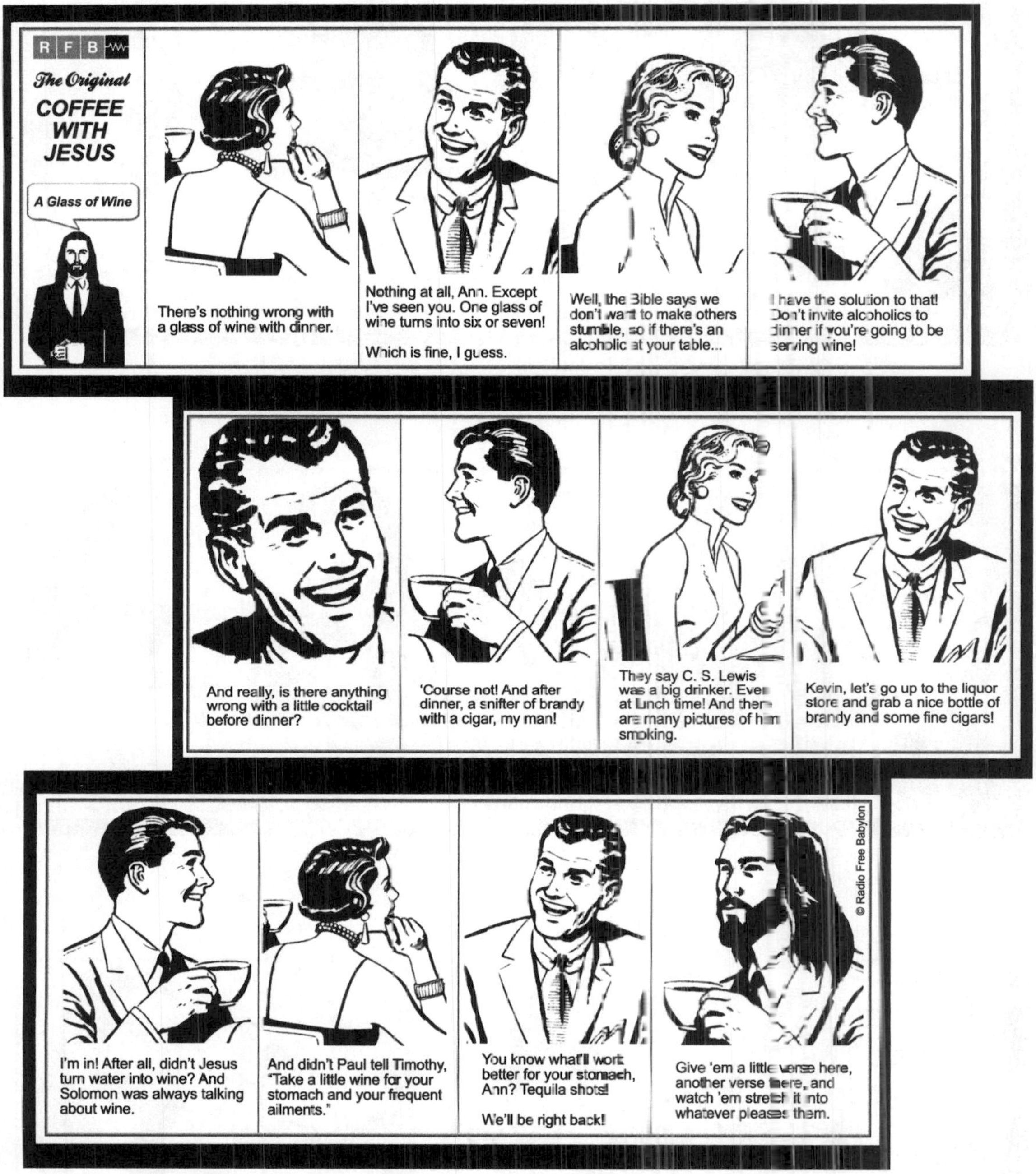
RFB
The Original
COFFEE WITH JESUS
A Glass of Wine
There's nothing wrong with a glass of wine with dinner.
Nothing at all, Ann. Except I've seen you. One glass of wine turns into six or seven!
Which is fine, I guess.
Well, the Bible says we don't want to make others stumble, so if there's an alcoholic at your table...
I have the solution to that! Don't invite alcoholics to dinner if you're going to be serving wine!
And really, is there anything wrong with a little cocktail before dinner?
'Course not! And after dinner, a snifter of brandy with a cigar, my man!
They say C. S. Lewis was a big drinker. Even at lunch time! And there are many pictures of him smoking.
Kevin, let's go up to the liquor store and grab a nice bottle of brandy and some fine cigars!
I'm in! After all, didn't Jesus turn water into wine? And Solomon was always talking about wine.
And didn't Paul tell Timothy, "Take a little wine for your stomach and your frequent ailments."
You know what'll work better for your stomach, Ann? Tequila shots!
We'll be right back!
Give 'em a little verse here, another verse there, and watch 'em stretch it into whatever pleases them.
© Radio Free Babylon

I Have No Free Will

You know my comings and my goings, right, Jesus?

You know everything about me, isn't that right?

Before a word is on your tongue, I know it completely, Ann. That's absolutely true.

What's your point?

That feels so *intrusive!*

It's like, I have no free will!

You know *before* I decide!

Just because I know what you're going to decide, Ann, doesn't mean I **make** you decide it.

© Radio Free Babylon

Swimming Pool

I think I've got a good analogy for the kingdom of God for this Sunday's sermon, Jesus.

A *river!*

It's been done so many times, Joe. It's obvious. "The current is the will of God. Don't swim upstream," etcetera.
I'd go with a swimming pool.

Okaaaay.

Any hints on how to elaborate?

"The kingdom of God is like unto a swimming pool. And most of you are splashing around in the shallow end."

© Radio Free Babylon

Very Few Will Share

I'll post about my business on Facebook, Jesus, and plenty of people will "like" my status, but very few will "share" it.

It's quite easy to simply "like" something, Carl, but there's a risk in sharing. It means they're putting their names behind it.

Wait...are you turning this into a lesson about the Gospel, Jesus?

Busted.

© Radio Free Babylon

Doing it Wrong

And if I *did* ever go back to church, Jesus, which of the twenty churches within a five-mile radius of my house would you recommend?

So you have options, Kevin.

Ya *think*? Proving how utterly confusing your faith is, Jesus! Everyone thinks the next guy is doing it wrong!

So, let's narrow your options, Kevin. Bypass all the ones who say everyone else is doing it wrong.

These Ordinary Skies

You lived so long ago, Jesus, and so distant from what we know today. It can sometimes feel like a fable. How can you really relate to us?

I lived as a human, Lisa, on this common earth, under these ordinary skies. The same sun made me squint; the same wind soothed me.

But did the same ignorant people get on your nerves and make you want to strangle them and then hide their bodies?

Your honesty is refreshing, Lisa.

Disturbing, to be sure, but refreshing nonetheless.

Heaven is For Real

I just loved the account from the little boy who said he visited heaven, Jesus. So inspiring.

It's true, right?

Only he and I will ever know, Ann.

Do you need it to be true?

I *want* to believe it's true, Jesus. I mean, if you can't trust a four-year-old, who *can* you trust?

Oh, I don't know...maybe the guy who said heaven is for real two thousand years ago?

© Radio Free Babylon

Opposite of Compassion

Sometimes, like in a crowded Walmart, I can get *so frustrated* with people. It's like I have **the opposite** of compassion. What's **wrong** with me, Jesus?

That place will try anyone's patience, Carl. For a better sense of your compassion, try visiting the pediatric ward of your local hospital.

Well, now you're just trying to make me cry, Jesus!

See?

You still got it, Carl.

So Outraged

Everyone is so **outraged**, Son of Man! All the time! It's 24/7! Outraged, offended and angry!

Mmm Mmm! Taste the *hate!*

You exaggerate, Satan.

It's not everyone, and it's not all the time.

Whatever!

Most everyone, **most** of the time! The point is *I'm winning*, Boy King!

Do you deceive even yourself, Satan? I mean, you've read the end of the story, right?

Head. Crushed.

Those Other Guys

I'm starting to agree on a few issues with those other guys, Jesus; the ones I was sure had a lot of Christianity wrong.

You do realize that this could be a career killer if it gets out to others in your denomination, right, Joe?

I've thought about that, Jesus, but I don't really consider ministry a *career*.

It's what I *have* to do.

Exactly the answer I was hoping for, Joe.

*Sooo...*how are your tent-making skills?

Come as You Are

They said, "Come as you are," Jesus, but it wasn't long before they started in with all the rules, the dos and don'ts, the attitude of judgment. I'd had enough.

In their zeal, people can sometimes take a heavy hand, Kevin. I'm sorry you had that experience. But was *I* ever like that with you?

Well, no, Jesus, but you could be awfully strong in your encouragement when you thought something in my life needed a change.

It's called growth, Kevin.

Come as you are, but don't stay as you came.

The Prayer Formula

I don't want to get the prayer formula wrong, Jesus. So, we're to pray to the *Father*, by the power of the *Spirit*, and *in your name*, right?

Thomas said to me, "My Lord and my God," Lisa. I was totally fine with that.

Don't worry about formulas.

I'm confused.

Just think of it as a conference call, Lisa.

We're all listening.

Prayer Rally

I'm going to that prayer rally to show my opposition against that thing, Jesus. Or my support for the opponents of that thing. Whatever.

Are they gathering in my name, Ann, or did they alert the press, issue statements and plan to make a scene for the sake of being seen?

This is *important*, Jesus!

How do you not *see* that?

A guy stands on the street corner making a great show of his devotion, Ann.

Ring any bells?

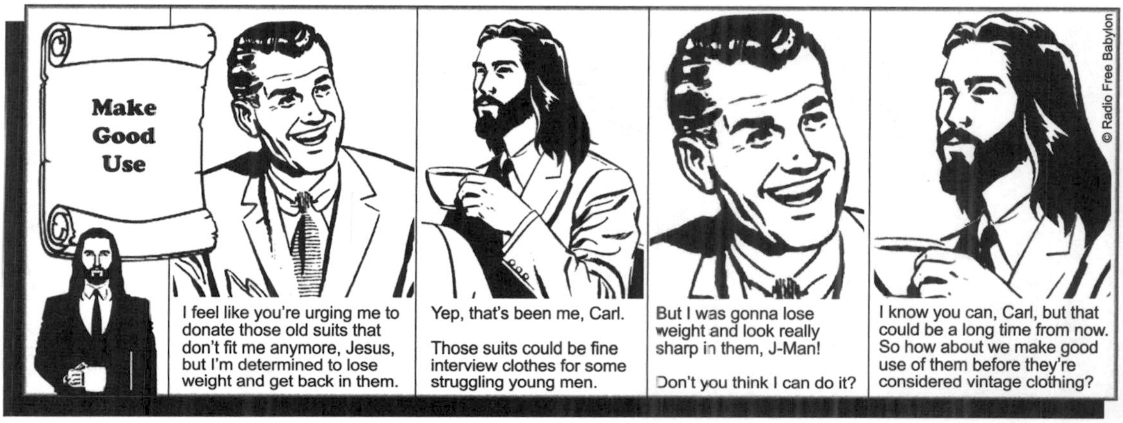
Make Good Use
I feel like you're urging me to donate those old suits that don't fit me anymore, Jesus, but I'm determined to lose weight and get back in them.
Yep, that's been me, Carl.
Those suits could be fine interview clothes for some struggling young men.
But I was gonna lose weight and look really sharp in them, J-Man!
Don't you think I can do it?
I know you can, Carl, but that could be a long time from now. So how about we make good use of them before they're considered vintage clothing?
© Radio Free Babylon

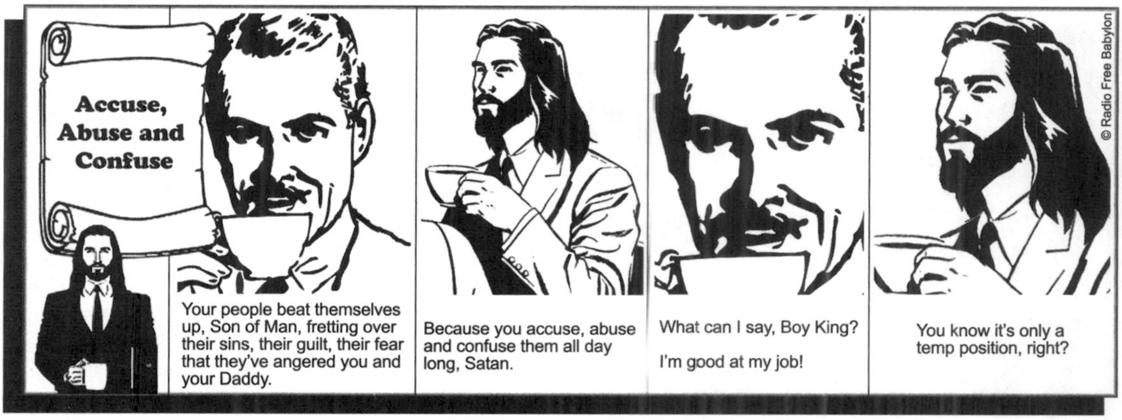
Accuse, Abuse and Confuse
Your people beat themselves up, Son of Man, fretting over their sins, their guilt, their fear that they've angered you and your Daddy.
Because you accuse, abuse and confuse them all day long, Satan.
What can I say, Boy King?
I'm good at my job!
You know it's only a temp position, right?
© Radio Free Babylon

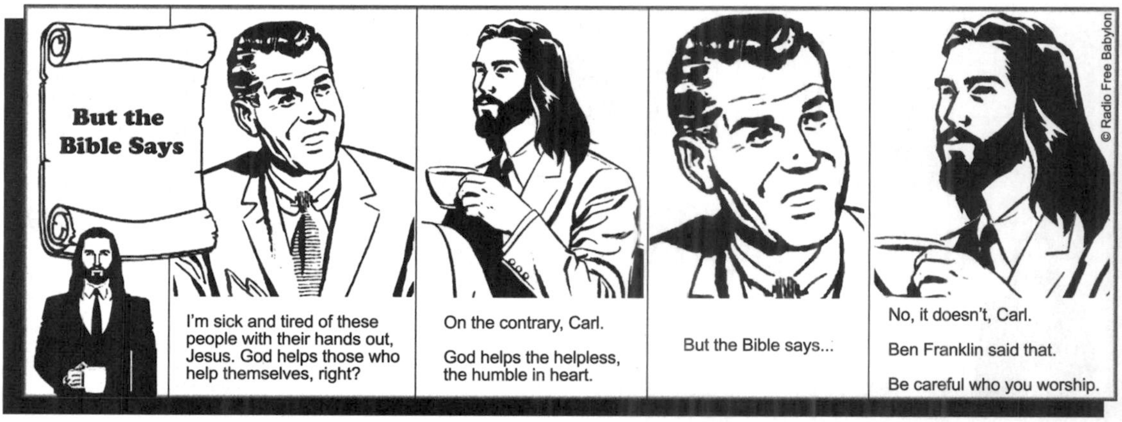
But the Bible Says
I'm sick and tired of these people with their hands out, Jesus. God helps those who help themselves, right?
On the contrary, Carl.
God helps the helpless, the humble in heart.
But the Bible says...
No, it doesn't, Carl.
Ben Franklin said that.
Be careful who you worship.
© Radio Free Babylon

Slow to Anger

OK, honest question here, Jesus: the Old Testament God seems mean and hateful, yet you're sweet and loving. Did you change your mind?

I don't change, Kevin. From the beginning, I have been *"compassionate, gracious, slow to anger, abounding in love and faithfulness."*

Ah ha! So the *"slow to anger"* clause is your out! And if you *"don't change,"* as you say, then maybe we'll see your anger again?

Let's just say nothing will go unreckoned, Kevin.

Doesn't Deserve It

I'm *not* forgiving him, Jesus!

He doesn't deserve it. And besides, he wouldn't even care if I did or didn't.

Let's let that statement hang out there for just a second, Ann.

I knew it was wrong as soon as it left my lips, Jesus. Who among us *deserves* forgiveness? I'm sorry.

And whether he cares or not, you're going to forgive him, Ann.

For your sake.

All Those Guys

I used to think of myself as a Wesleyan, but I'm probably more of a Calvinist, really.

Calvinism was too severe for me. I identify more with Arminiansim.

I love the Franciscans, but I found Lutheranism to be a more comfortable fit.

I love all those guys... but I just wanted Jesus people.

© Radio Free Babylon

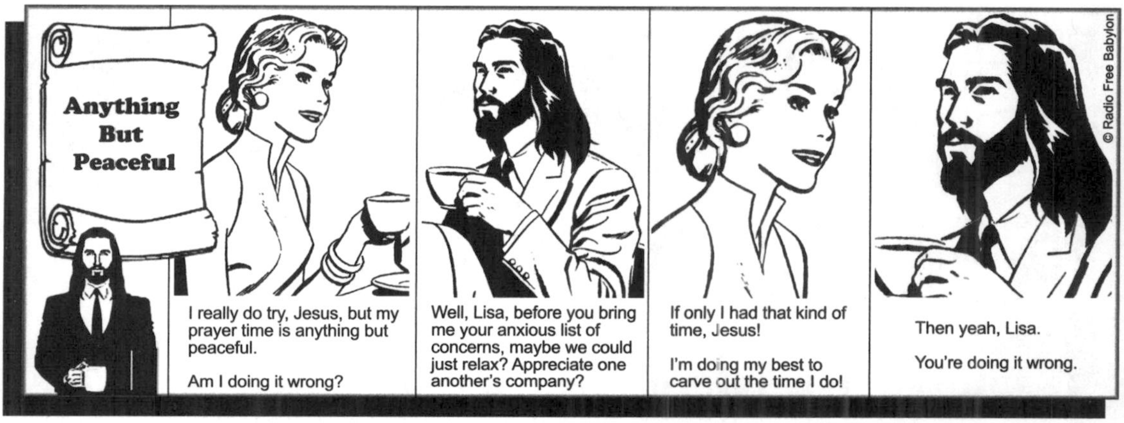
Anything But Peaceful
© Radio Free Babylon
I really do try, Jesus, but my prayer time is anything but peaceful.
Am I doing it wrong?
Well, Lisa, before you bring me your anxious list of concerns, maybe we could just relax? Appreciate one another's company?
If only I had that kind of time, Jesus!
I'm doing my best to carve out the time I do!
Then yeah, Lisa.
You're doing it wrong.

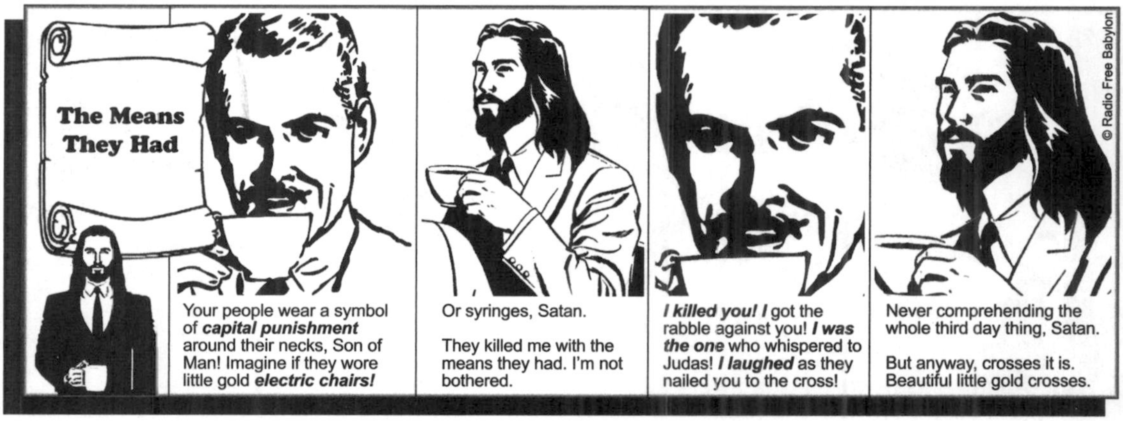
The Means They Had
© Radio Free Babylon
Your people wear a symbol of ***capital punishment*** around their necks, Son of Man! Imagine if they wore little gold ***electric chairs!***
Or syringes, Satan.
They killed me with the means they had. I'm not bothered.
I killed you! I got the rabble against you! ***I was the one*** who whispered to Judas! ***I laughed*** as they nailed you to the cross!
Never comprehending the whole third day thing, Satan.
But anyway, crosses it is. Beautiful little gold crosses.

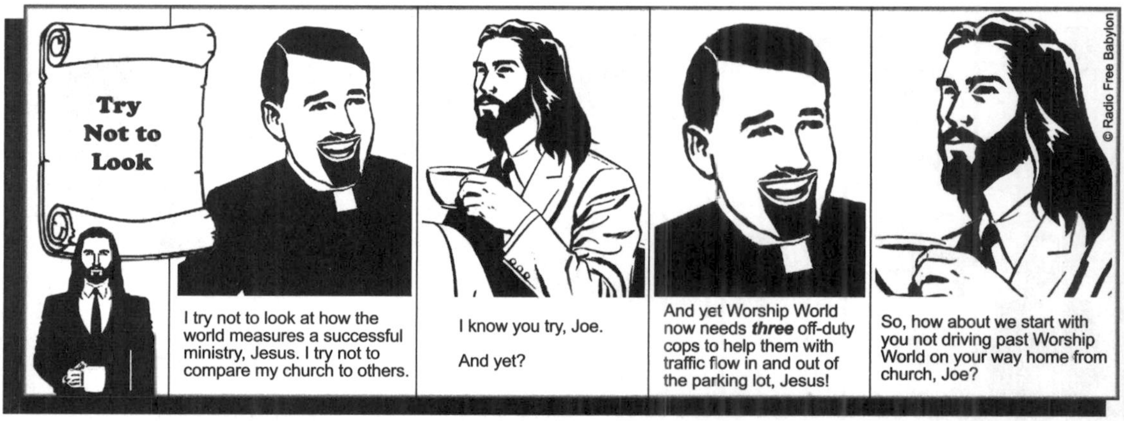
Try Not to Look
© Radio Free Babylon
I try not to look at how the world measures a successful ministry, Jesus. I try not to compare my church to others.
I know you try, Joe.
And yet?
And yet Worship World now needs ***three*** off-duty cops to help them with traffic flow in and out of the parking lot, Jesus!
So, how about we start with you not driving past Worship World on your way home from church, Joe?

Spoiled Rotten Babies

Forgive me, Jesus, but I just can't help viewing some in my congregation as a bunch of spoiled rotten babies.

I hear ya, Joe. Impatient complainers, always seeing the negative, not happy unless everything is going their way? They're a pain.

knew you saw it the same way, Jesus! Thanks for understand...

..or, crap.

Yeah, I forgive you.

Looked Around & Got Scared

I like to think that if I was in that boat and saw you walking on the water, I'd have stepped out and run to you without a hint of sinking, Jesus.

I know you like to think that, Carl, but the reality is that you'd have done just as Peter did; looked around and got scared.

C'mon Jesus! Those guys lived with you night and day for three years! They should've known by then what you could do!

And you're going on four decades, Carl, still not quite convinced.

Make It So

Jesus, I am your faithful servant.

I hope so, Lisa.

Well, don't just *hope so*, Jesus.

Make it so!

Ah, but that's where *you* come in, Lisa.

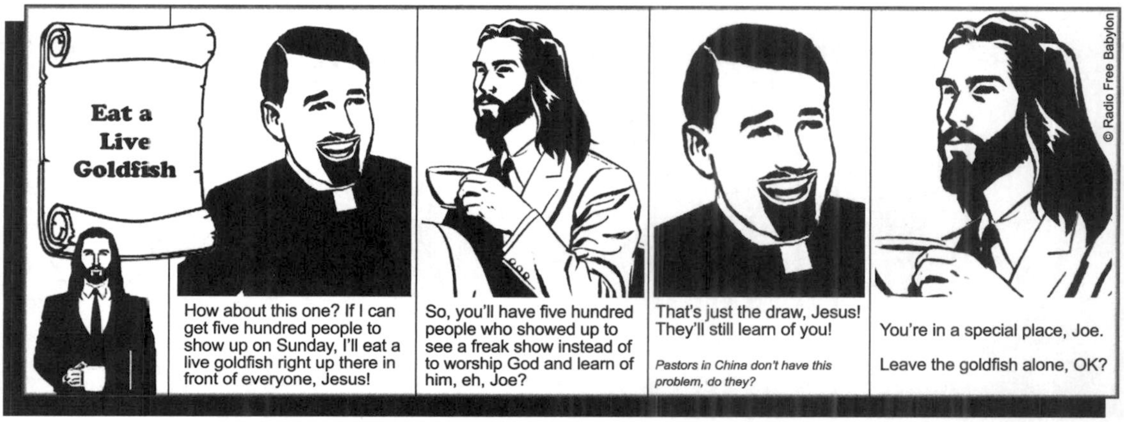
Eat a Live Goldfish
How about this one? If I can get five hundred people to show up on Sunday, I'll eat a live goldfish right up there in front of everyone, Jesus!
So, you'll have five hundred people who showed up to see a freak show instead of to worship God and learn of him, eh, Joe?
That's just the draw, Jesus! They'll still learn of you!
Pastors in China don't have this problem, do they?
You're in a special place, Joe.
Leave the goldfish alone, OK?
© Radio Free Babylon

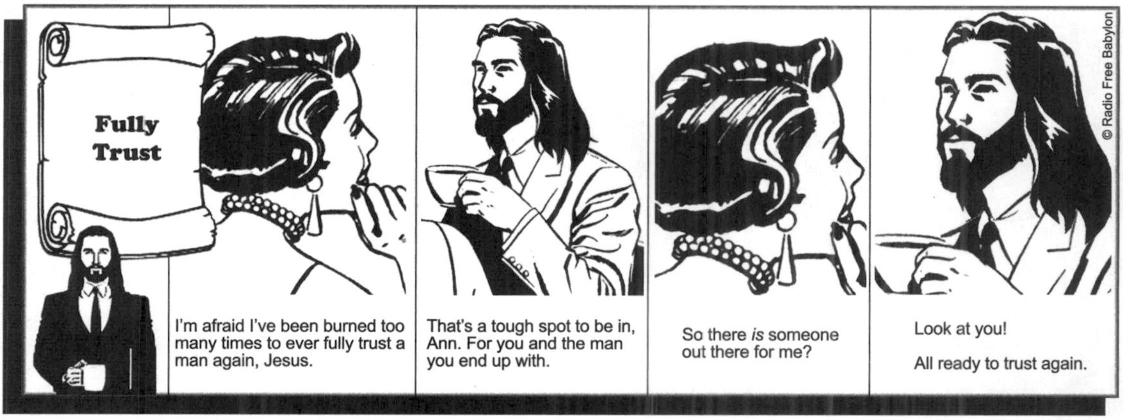
Fully Trust
I'm afraid I've been burned too many times to ever fully trust a man again, Jesus.
That's a tough spot to be in, Ann. For you and the man you end up with.
So there *is* someone out there for me?
Look at you!
All ready to trust again.
© Radio Free Babylon

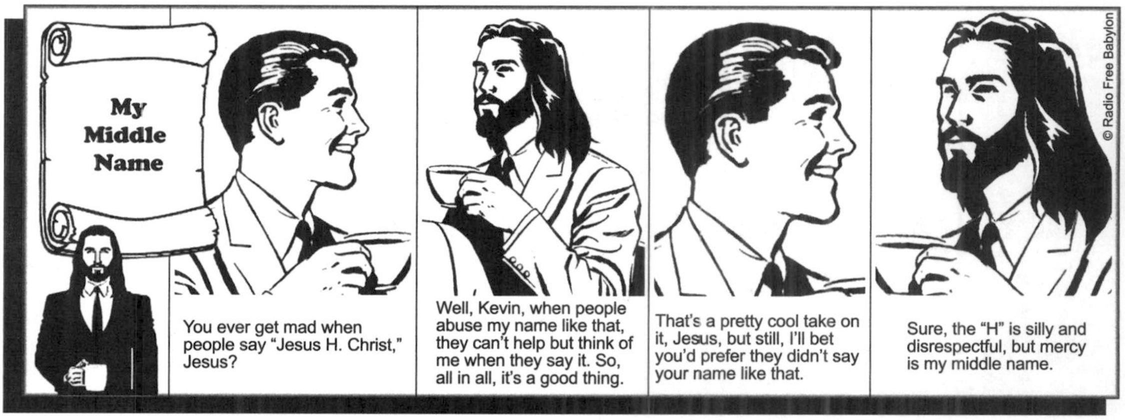
My Middle Name
You ever get mad when people say "Jesus H. Christ," Jesus?
Well, Kevin, when people abuse my name like that, they can't help but think of me when they say it. So, all in all, it's a good thing.
That's a pretty cool take on it, Jesus, but still, I'll bet you'd prefer they didn't say your name like that.
Sure, the "H" is silly and disrespectful, but mercy is my middle name.
© Radio Free Babylon

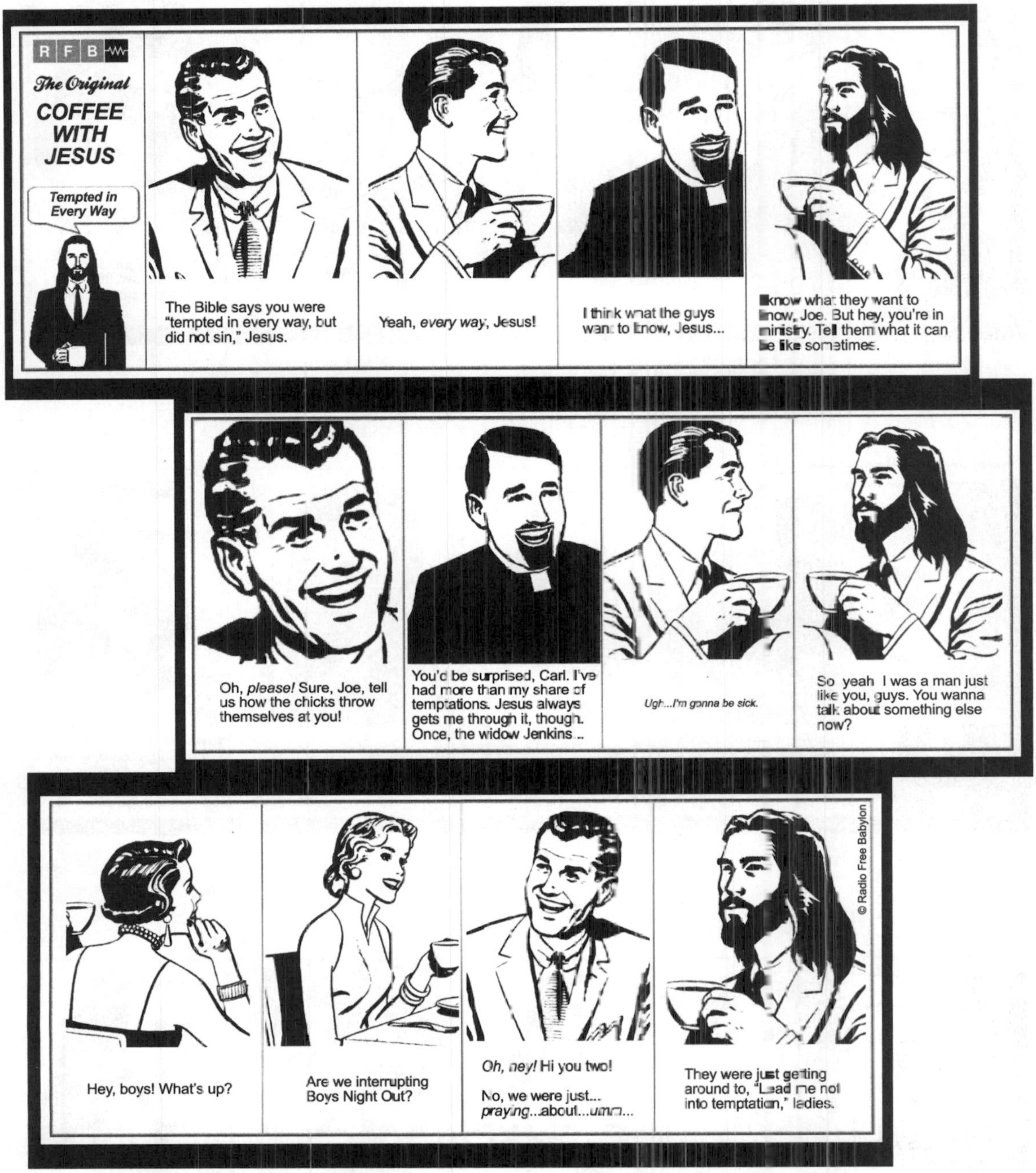
RFB
The Original
COFFEE WITH JESUS
Tempted in Every Way
The Bible says you were "tempted in every way, but did not sin," Jesus.
Yeah, *every way*, Jesus!
I think what the guys want to know, Jesus...
I know what they want to know, Joe. But hey, you're in ministry. Tell them what it can be like sometimes.
Oh, *please!* Sure, Joe, tell us how the chicks throw themselves at you!
You'd be surprised, Carl. I've had more than my share of temptations. Jesus always gets me through it, though. Once, the widow Jenkins...
Ugh...I'm gonna be sick.
So yeah I was a man just like you, guys. You wanna talk about something else now?
Hey, boys! What's up?
Are we interrupting Boys Night Out?
Oh, hey! Hi you two!
No, we were just... *praying*...about...*umm*...
They were just getting around to, "Lead me not into temptation," ladies.
© Radio Free Babylon

The Next World

Self-confidence is key if you want to get ahead in this world, Jesus.

And what if you want to get ahead in the next world, Carl?

Are you trying to tell me I can't have success in this life if I want to go to heaven?

I was actually just telling you to dial down the self-confidence a notch, Carl.

A Little Formal

Too many of my people see prayer as a chore, drudgery.

How can I help them get past that, Jesus?

Have you listened to yourself pray in front of them, Joe? It's a little formal; not like when it's just you and me.

Wow. So my prayers from the pulpit and in counseling are...stuffy?

Prayer should feel like your favorite, threadbare, loose fitting, cotton t-shirt, Joe. Yours sound a lot more like a polyester three-piece suit.

Here in the West

Take away the stained glass, the comfortable seating, the air-conditioning, Son of Man, how many do you suppose would show up?

There are congregations gathering in the open air, Satan, to say nothing of run-down, hot and dusty meeting spaces.

You know what I meant! *Here*, in the West, Boy King!

They would fall away *en masse* without their luxury!

Perhaps we'll see.

In the Woodshed

Why do I always feel like I'm in the woodshed with you, Jesus; like I'm getting disciplined?

Those whom I love I rebuke and discipline, Carl. And some, not mentioning any names, need that more than others.

So, I'm like a problem child; the bad kid?

You can look at it as having to stay after class, Carl.

Or...you get extra one-on-one time with the Teacher.

In a Cult

When I look at the book of Acts and how the first church did things, Jesus, selling their homes, pooling their money; it's like they were in a cult!

From your comfortable perch, Carl, I'm sure it can look that way. But you have to consider the time, the place, the circumstances.

There's really no two ways about it, Jesus.

It was Communism!

No, Carl.

It was Community.

Soul Check

Sometimes, I'll be about to do something, say something or maybe even write something, then I'll do a soul-check and stop myself, Jesus.

Thinking, "Who does this help? Who might this hurt? Am I just being vain? What's the point? Is it better left undone, unsaid, unwritten?"

Exactly! Wow, it's like you're *in my mind.* So, that's *you* asking the questions and making me stop myself, Jesus.

It's me asking the questions, Lisa, but it's you stopping yourself.

Couldn't do it without you.

© Radio Free Babylon

Just Unload

I'm not where I thought I'd be, Jesus. I was going to *win souls! Shake the rafters* with my preaching! *Move mountains* with my prayers!

I'm. I. I'd. I. My. My.

Don't you think I already know how selfish that sounded, Jesus? Am I not allowed to be *honest* with you? Can't I just *unload?*

By all means, Joe, please.

Empty yourself.

Called But Not Chosen

So why didn't it stick for me, Jesus? Was I not one of your "elect?" Am I one of the many who are "called," but not "chosen?"

The invitation's still out there, Kevin.

Ehhh...

So, you've chosen.

Grueling Slog

Eternity is a long, long time, Jesus.

That's not really how it works, Ann. Eternity is timeless. It's not like you'll be watching a clock. Trust me, you'll love it.

But the whole concept of immortality...*forever*...I just don't know if I'm up for that sort of grueling slog. Will we at least get to take naps?

I know somebody who needs one right now.

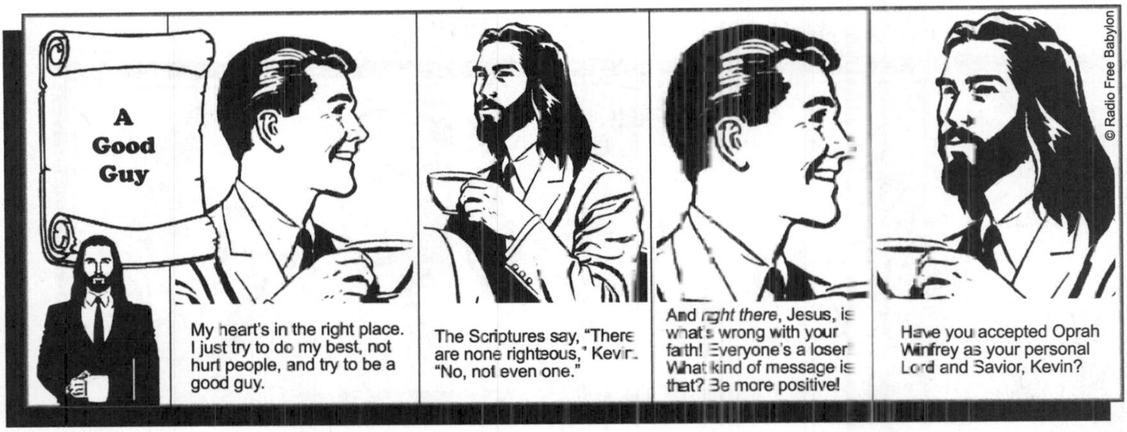
A Good Guy
My heart's in the right place. I just try to do my best, not hurt people, and try to be a good guy.
The Scriptures say, "There are none righteous," Kevin. "No, not even one."
And *right there*, Jesus, is what's wrong with your faith! Everyone's a loser! What kind of message is that? Be more positive!
Have you accepted Oprah Winfrey as your personal Lord and Savior, Kevin?
© Radio Free Babylon

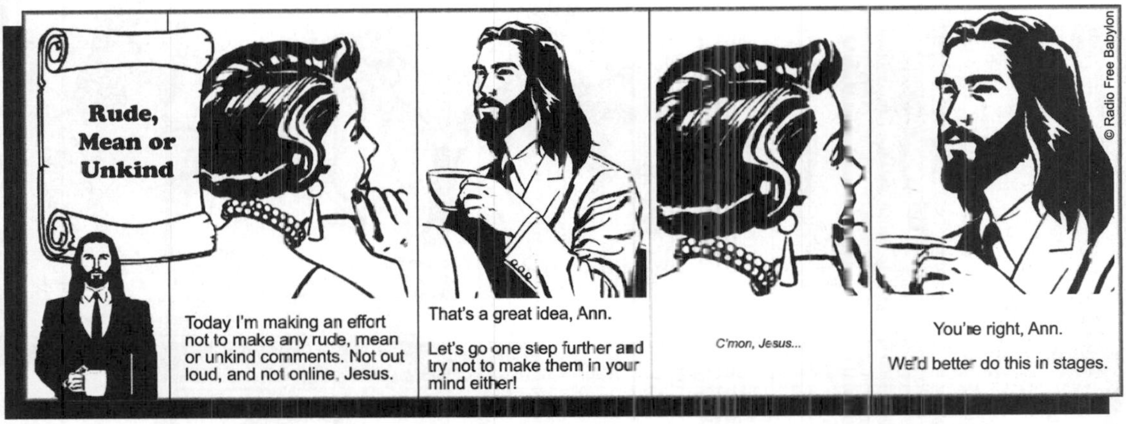
Rude, Mean or Unkind
Today I'm making an effort not to make any rude, mean or unkind comments. Not out loud, and not online, Jesus.
That's a great idea, Ann.
Let's go one step further and try not to make them in your mind either!
C'mon, Jesus...
You're right, Ann.
We'd better do this in stages.
© Radio Free Babylon

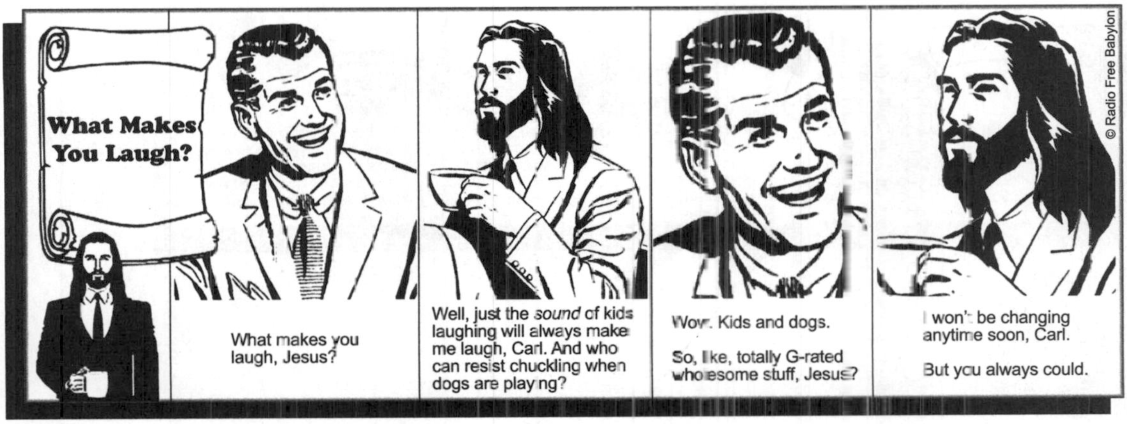
What Makes You Laugh?
What makes you laugh, Jesus?
Well, just the *sound* of kids laughing will always make me laugh, Carl. And who can resist chuckling when dogs are playing?
Wow. Kids and dogs.
So, like, totally G-rated wholesome stuff, Jesus?
I won't be changing anytime soon, Carl.
But you always could.
© Radio Free Babylon

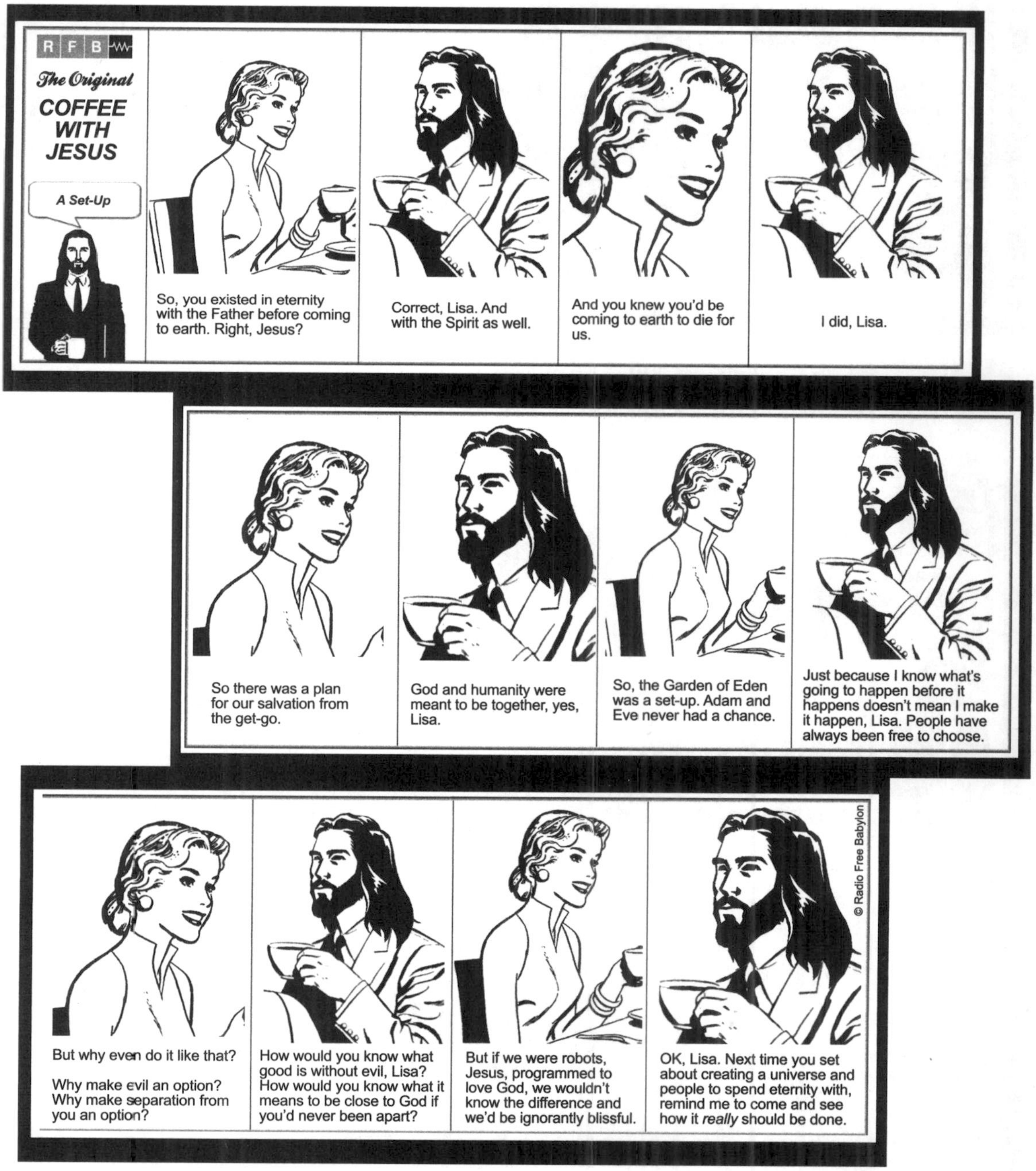
R F B
The Original
COFFEE WITH JESUS
A Set-Up
So, you existed in eternity with the Father before coming to earth. Right, Jesus?
Correct, Lisa. And with the Spirit as well.
And you knew you'd be coming to earth to die for us.
I did, Lisa.
So there was a plan for our salvation from the get-go.
God and humanity were meant to be together, yes, Lisa.
So, the Garden of Eden was a set-up. Adam and Eve never had a chance.
Just because I know what's going to happen before it happens doesn't mean I make it happen, Lisa. People have always been free to choose.
But why even do it like that?
Why make evil an option? Why make separation from you an option?
How would you know what good is without evil, Lisa? How would you know what it means to be close to God if you'd never been apart?
But if we were robots, Jesus, programmed to love God, we wouldn't know the difference and we'd be ignorantly blissful.
OK, Lisa. Next time you set about creating a universe and people to spend eternity with, remind me to come and see how it *really* should be done.
© Radio Free Babylon

One of the many goals of Radio Free Babylon is to make people laugh and think—not always in that order and not always simultaneously. This book has hopefully done both of those for you.

We have other plans and means (some of them realized, others still in the planning stages) for continuing to reach people where they live, leaving them scratching their heads or chuckling. Or both. Learn more at

RadioFreeBabylon.com

Also Available from InterVarsity Press

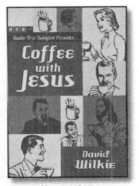

Coffee with Jesus
978-0-8308-3662-8

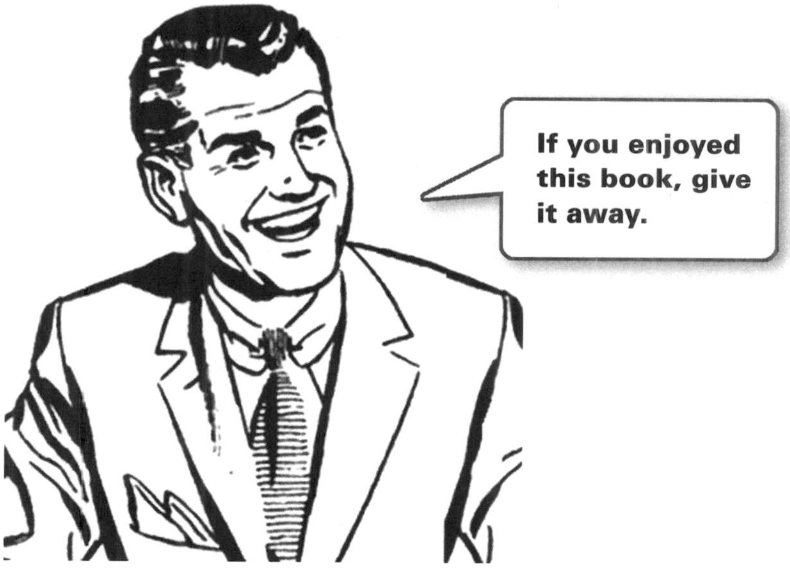
If you enjoyed this book, give it away.

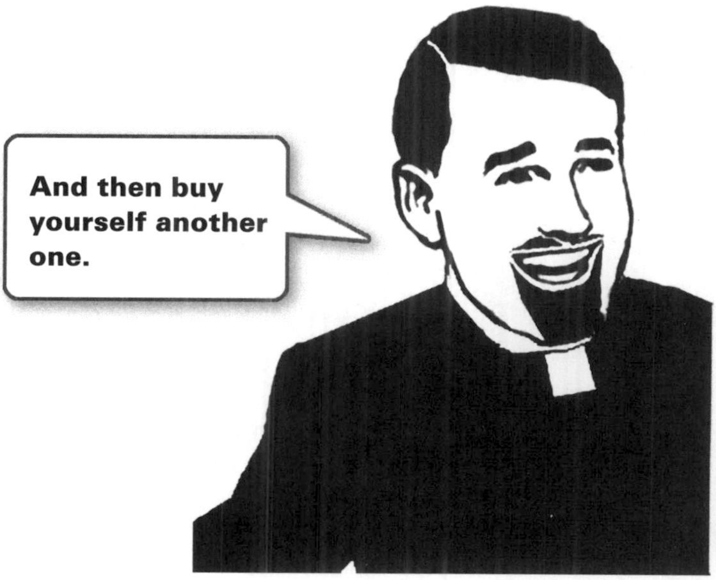
And then buy yourself another one.